The Perks of Being a Wallflower

FADE IN:

EXT. TUNNEL - NIGHT

      The titles begin over black. We hear the sound of an old
      typewriter. Someone reaching out to us. The bell dings,
      announcing the end of a line, and we see our title...

      THE PERKS *OF* **BEING** *A* WALLFLOWER

      Music begins, picture fades up, and we are in the city.
      Downtown Pittsburgh. Looking out of the back window like a
      child in the back of a station wagon.

      We see lights on buildings and everything that makes us
      wonder. We see the bridge. And the river below. And then
      we enter...

      The Tunnel.

      We keep moving backwards, watching the lights. Golden,
      alive, and hypnotic. The music carries us as we float out of
      the tunnel. Onto another bridge. And over the highway.

      We move into the night sky, back through the trees, through a
      window, and into...

INT. CHARLIE'S BEDROOM - NIGHT

      It is a neat and tidy little room. Few posters or books.
      CHARLIE is 15. He is innocent, hopeful, awkward, and likable
      to everyone but his classmates. He sits at his desk, writing
      a letter in pencil as he tapes the title song through the
      radio on his cassette boom box.

                          CHARLIE (V.O.)
                Dear Friend, I am writing to you because
                she said you listen and understand and
                didn't try to sleep with that person at
                that party even though you could have.
                Please don't try to figure out who she is
                because then you might figure out who I
                am, and I don't want you to do that. I
                just need to know that people like you
                exist. Like if you met me, you wouldn't
                think I was the weird kid who spent time
                in the hospital. And I wouldn't make you
                nervous.

INT. CHARLIE'S HOUSE - MOMENTS LATER

      Charlie anxiously walks through the hallway of his suburban
      split level house.

> CHARLIE (V.O.)
> I hope it's okay for me to think that.
> You see, I haven't really talked to
> anyone outside of my family all summer.

Charlie moves to the living room where dad watches a football game. Mom reads a page turner and sips her white wine. Charlie waits for them to notice him. And waits. And waits.

4   INT. CHARLIE'S BEDROOM - NIGHT   4

Charlie sits at his desk, continuing his letter in pencil.

> CHARLIE (V.O.)
> But tomorrow is my first day of high
> school ever, and I really need to turn
> things around this year.
>   (hopeful)
> So, I have a plan.

5   INT. MILL GROVE HIGH SCHOOL HALLWAY - LAST DAY   5

We see it in Charlie's mind. Slow motion and wondrous. The kids clear out their lockers by throwing their old papers in the air like a New York confetti parade.

> CHARLIE (V.O.)
> As I enter the school for the first time,
> I will visualize what it will be like on
> the last day of my senior year.

Charlie walks down the hall. Triumphant. Confident. Happy.

> CHARLIE (V.O.) (CONT'D)
> Unfortunately, I counted, and that's...

                                                      SMASH CUT TO:

6   INT. MILL GROVE HIGH SCHOOL HALLWAY - FIRST DAY   6

Reality. The bell rings, and we see the chaotic maze from Charlie's POV. A SENIOR BULLY leads the ritual, making dozens of freshmen hop down the hall.

> SENIOR BULLY
> Hop, freshman toads. Hop! Move it, boys!

As seniors grab more victims, Charlie moves to the wall.

> CHARLIE (V.O.)
> ... 1,385 days from now.

VARSITY FOOTBALL PLAYERS pass, wearing their letter jackets.

                         LINEBACKER
                Man, you got big.

                         NOSE TACKLE
                Worked out all summer. Rock hard, dude.

At the front of the pack is **BRAD HAYS** (17), the quarterback.
He's good looking, charismatic, and friendly. The big man on
campus. Nice guy, too.

                         BRAD HAYS
                Would you guys get a room?

They laugh. Charlie turns to the trophy case to avoid them.
Trying to make himself as small as possible.

                         CHARLIE (V.O.)
                    (trying to be optimistic)
                Just 1,385 days.

7   INT. MILL GROVE HIGH SCHOOL - CAFETERIA - LUNCH   7

Charlie moves down the lunch line with his sister. **CANDACE
KELMECKIS** is 17 and a beautiful type A, straight A priss.

                         CHARLIE (V.O.)
                In the meantime, I'd hoped that my sister
                Candace and her boyfriend Derek would
                have let me eat lunch with their earth
                club.

                         CANDACE
                Seniors only.
                    (barks to Derek)
                What are you doing with a plastic spork?

Candace turns to her boyfriend, **DEREK**, 17. Derek is such a
pussy, the most masculine thing about him is his pony-tail.

                         DEREK
                I don't want to bring back silverware--

                         CANDACE
                Derek, you're Earth Club Treasurer.

Derek takes the silverware like a beaten dog. Charlie
watches them move into the intimidating cafeteria.

8   INT. CAFETERIA - LATER   8

Charlie sits in the corner alone, observing everyone having a
great time with their friends. He sees a pretty girl with
blonde hair having the best first day. This is **SUSAN**, 14.

> CHARLIE (V.O.)
> When my sister said no, I thought maybe
> my old friend Susan would want to have
> lunch with me.

Charlie catches her eye and waves, but she looks away.

> CHARLIE (V.O.) (CONT'D)
> In middle school, Susan was very fun to
> be around, but now she doesn't like to
> say hi to me anymore.

Charlie turns his attention to the quarterback, Brad Hays.

> CHARLIE (V.O.) (CONT'D)
> And then there's Brad Hays, who's the
> quarterback of our team. Before my
> brother went to play football for Penn
> State, he and Brad played together. So,
> I thought maybe he'd say hi to me. But
> Brad's a senior, and I'm me, so... who am
> I kidding?

Brad catches Charlie staring at him. Awkward.

9   INT. SHOP CLASS - DAY   9

Charlie sits by himself, watching the freshmen boys laugh as
a senior paints a goatee on his face with a grease pencil.

> CHARLIE (V.O.)
> On the bright side, one senior decided to
> make fun of the teacher instead of the
> freshmen. He even drew on Mr. Callahan's
> legendary goatee with a grease pencil.

Meet **PATRICK** (18), full of confidence, mischief, and so over
high school. He is the class clown, performing a perfect
imitation of the teacher, Mr. Callahan.

> PATRICK
> Boys, the prick punch is not a toy. I
> learned that in 'Nam back in '68.
> "Callahan," the sergeant said, "put down
> that prick punch and go kill some gooks."

The laughter suddenly dies as the real **MR. CALLAHAN** (57)
walks up behind the oblivious Patrick.

> PATRICK (CONT'D)
> But you know what happened? That prick
> punch killed my best friend in a Saigon
> whorehouse.

Patrick suddenly feels Mr. Callahan behind him. Oops.

                    MR. CALLAHAN
          I heard you were going to be in my class.
          Are you proud being a senior taking
          freshman shop, Patty-Cakes?

                    PATRICK
          My name is Patrick. You call me Patrick
          or you call me nothing.

                    MR. CALLAHAN
          Okay... Nothing.

The class laughs. Except Charlie. He watches Patrick take
the long walk back to his seat.

                    CHARLIE (V.O.)
          I felt really bad for Patrick. He wasn't
          saying the impersonation to be mean or
          anything. He was just trying to make us
          freshmen feel better.

                    MR. CALLAHAN
          Everyone open your safety guides.
          Nothing... why don't you read first?

Patrick opens the book.

                    PATRICK
          Chapter 1. Surviving your fascist shop
          teacher, who needs to put kids down to
          feel big.
               (to the class)
          Oh, wow. This is useful guys. We should
          read on.

Charlie smiles. He loves him already.

10   INT. ENGLISH CLASS - MORNING   10

The kids pass back paperback copies of To Kill A Mockingbird.
Charlie opens his Trapper Keeper, takes a pencil out of the
plastic pouch, and writes... "ENGLISH CLASS... DAY ONE."

                    CHARLIE (V.O.)
          My last class of the day is advanced
          English, and I'm excited to finally start
          learning with the smartest kids in the
          school...

A **SMART ASS FRESHMAN** girl with braces smiles at him.

                    SMART ASS FRESHMAN
                         (whispers)
              Nice Trapper Keeper, faggot.

The kids around him laugh. Charlie's ears turn red. At the
blackboard, the teacher writes his name... Mr. Anderson. But
you can call him **BILL** (27). Bill is an idealist.

                         BILL
              Shhh. I'm Mr. Anderson. And thanks to
              Teach for America, I'm going to be your
              teacher for freshman English. This
              semester, we're going to be learning
              Harper Lee's To Kill a Mockingbird.
              Genius book. Now, who wants to get out
              of the first pop quiz?

All hands go up. Except Charlie's. Bill paces the rows.

                         BILL (CONT'D)
              I'm shocked. Alright. You can skip the
              quiz if you tell me which author invented
              the paperback book. Anyone?

As kids think, Bill confiscates contraband, removes hats.

                         BILL (CONT'D)
              He's British. He also invented the
              serial. In fact, at the end of chapter 3
              of his first novel, he had a man hanging
              off a cliff by his fingernails. Hence,
              the term cliffhanger. Anybody?

                         FRESHMAN GIRL
              Shakespeare.

                         BILL
              That's a great guess, but no, Shakespeare
              didn't write novels. Anybody else?
                         (off their silence)
              The author was...

Bill is about to give the answer when he notices Charlie has
already written... **Charles Dickens.**

                         BILL (CONT'D)
              ... Charles Dickens. However, if you and
              I had gone to a play in Shakespeare's
              time, it would have cost 4 pennies. Can
              you imagine that? We would have put
              those pennies in a metal box, which the
              ushers would lock in the office. And
              that's where we get the term... anyone?

                    KIDS (O.S.)
        "Office Depot!" "Office Supplies!"

Charlie writes down **Box Office**, then looks up to find that
Bill is staring at him. Waiting for him to raise his hand.

                    BILL
        I'll give you a free "A" on anything but
        the final term paper if you get it right.

Charlie looks down. He's not going to answer.

                    BILL (CONT'D)
        <u>Box</u> <u>office</u>.

The kids groan. They should have known. Charlie smiles to
himself. He's going to like this class.

11   INT. ENGLISH CLASS - LATER   11

The bell rings. The students chatter their way out of class.
The last to leave is Charlie.

                    BILL
        You should learn to participate.

Charlie stops and turns to find Bill erasing the board.

                    BILL (CONT'D)
        Why didn't you raise your hand?
            (off Charlie's shrug)
        They call you teacher's pet? Freak?
            (off Charlie's nod)
        I used to get spaz. I mean, come on,
        <u>spaz</u>?

Charlie smiles. Bill takes a moment. Then...

                    BILL (CONT'D)
        So, I heard you had a tough time last
        year. But they say if you make one friend
        on your first day, you're doing okay.

                    CHARLIE
        Thank you, sir, but if my English teacher
        is the only friend I make today, that
        would be sort of depressing.

                    BILL
        Yeah. I could see that.

                    CHARLIE
        Don't worry, Mr. Anderson. I'm okay.

Bill nods and watches Charlie exit. He gets swallowed up by the hallway as the bell rings.

12   INT. MILL GROVE HIGH SCHOOL - HALLWAY - DAY   12

Charlie looks through the thick office glass. He sees Patrick use his charms on MRS. SMALL, (58) the Principal.

                    PATRICK
               (to Mrs. Small)
          I would happily not take shop...

Out of nowhere, the SENIOR BULLY grabs Charlie's book.

                    SENIOR BULLY
          Hey, Freshman Toad.

The bully rips the cover. He throws it on the ground as his friends laugh and disappear down the hall. Charlie walks up and picks up his book.

                    CHARLIE (V.O.)
          Well, I have 1,384 days to go. And just
          so I say it to someone, high school is
          even worse than middle school.

13   EXT. CHARLIE'S HOUSE - DAY   13

Charlie walks up the path to his house.

                    CHARLIE (V.O.)
          If my parents ask me about it, I probably
          won't tell them the truth because I don't
          want them to worry that I might get bad
          again.

14   INT. CHARLIE'S HOUSE - AFTERNOON   14

Charlie tapes his book cover back together. He looks up as his dad comes home from a long day. Charlie's mom hugs him.

                    CHARLIE (V.O.)
          If my Aunt Helen were still here, I could
          talk to her. And I know she would
          understand how I am both happy and sad,
          and I'm still trying to figure out how
          that could be. I just hope I make a
          friend soon. Love always, Charlie.

15   INT. CHARLIE'S DINING ROOM - EARLY EVENING   15

Charlie stands in the kitchen, pouring his milk.

                         MOTHER (O.S.)
                  Charlie, come on.

His family is seated around the table. Candace's boyfriend,
Derek, is their special guest.

                         DEREK
                  Mmmm. This chicken paprikash is
                  delicious, Mrs. Kelmeckis.

Charlie's father rolls his eyes, then reads his sports page.

                         MOTHER
                  Thank you, Derek. It's Charlie's
                  favorite. He was a little nervous about
                  starting high school, so I made it.

                         FATHER
                  You feel a little silly being nervous
                  now, huh, champ?

                         CHARLIE
                  Yes, sir. I sure do.

Charlie carries his milk back to the table. He quickly sits,
hoping someone will change the subject.

                         FATHER
                  I told you. Just give 'em a smile and be
                  yourself. That's how you--

                         CANDACE
                  "--make friends in the real world."

                         FATHER
                  You're cruisin' for a bruisin'.

                         DEREK
                  Freshman year is tough, but you really
                  find yourself.

                         FATHER
                       (deep eye roll)
                  Thanks, Derek.

16   INT. LIVING ROOM / ENTRY HALL - EVENING   16

Charlie's father and mother watch a local sports show.
Charlie passes by them with ice cream on his way downstairs.

                         MOTHER
                  I think you could be a little nicer to
                  Derek.

FATHER
I'm sorry. The kid's a pussy. I can't
stand him.

Charlie moves to the entry hall. He looks through the screen
door to the porch where Candace kisses Derek's cheek goodbye.
As Derek walks to his mom's Mercedes, Candace joins Charlie.

DEREK
(waving from car)
I hope you love the mix I made. The
cover is hand-painted.

When he gets into his car, she hands Charlie the mix tape.

CANDACE
Charlie, do you want this?

CHARLIE
Are you sure?

CANDACE
He gives me one every week.

17   INT. CHARLIE'S BED ROOM - DUSK   17

Charlie sits on his bed, reading To Kill a Mockingbird, the
cover taped back together. We see Derek's mix... Autumn
Leaves... rotate in his old tape recorder.

DEREK (V.O.)
Hey, Babe. This next one might be a
little sad, but it reminded me of your
eyes.

The first notes of The Smiths' "Asleep" begins. As Morrissey
sings, Charlie keeps reading. And reading.

CUT TO:

18   INT. CHARLIE'S BEDROOM - DAY   18

The reading is done. Charlie proudly puts To Kill a
Mockingbird on his newly dubbed "Shelf of Fame."

19   INT. MILL GROVE HIGH SCHOOL - HALLWAY - AFTERNOON   19

The songs continues as we see glimpses of Charlie's day to
day life over the next few weeks. Charlie exits his English
class. FRESHMEN BULLIES wait for him, led by...

SMART ASS FRESHMAN
Did you already do the term paper on To

Silence. They grab and drag him into the boy's room. We
hear the toilet flush for the swirly.

20   INT. CHARLIE'S BEDROOM - DUSK   20

Charlie looks at the new bottle of prescription Wellbutrin.
He puts a pill in his mouth and washes it down with RC cola.

21   INT. CHARLIE'S LIVING ROOM - AFTERNOON   21

Charlie watches his brother and the Penn State Nittany Lions
on TV. He looks over at his father, but his dad is too busy
building Charlie's clock for shop class to notice him.

22   INT. MILL GROVE HIGH SCHOOL - CAFETERIA - LUNCH   22

Charlie carries his tray through the intimidating cafeteria.
Not giving up. Looking for somewhere to sit.

                                                        CUT TO:

23   INT. MILL GROVE HIGH SCHOOL - CAFETERIA - LUNCH   23

Charlie sits by himself in the corner. He looks around the
cafeteria, wanting to break in. Not knowing how. After a
moment, he returns to his book. The song ends.

24   EXT. MILL GROVE HIGH SCHOOL - FOOTBALL STADIUM - NIGHT   24

Friday Night Football in Western, PA. Charlie buys his Coke
and nachos and wanders to the bleachers. He sits alone,
trying to blend in by cheering with the rest of students.
When the Mill Grove Devils recover a fumble, he hears...

                        PATRICK
              Come on Devils! Woooooo!

Charlie looks up at Patrick, cheering his head off. **TWIN
SENIOR GIRLS** pass him, taunting.

                    TWIN SENIOR GIRLS
              Hey, Nothing. Hey, Nothing.

                        PATRICK
              Suck it, virginity pledges!

Charlie wants to go up to Patrick so badly. After driving
himself crazy, sitting up and down twice, he approaches.

                        CHARLIE
              Hey... Patrick.

                    PATRICK
          Hey! You're in my shop class, right?
          How's your clock coming?

                    CHARLIE
          My dad's building it.

                    PATRICK
          Yeah. Mine looks like a boat.
              (off Charlie's awkward silence)
          You want to sit over here, or are you
          waiting for your friends?

                    CHARLIE
          No. I'll sit if that's okay.

Patrick motions for Charlie to sit. Charlie sits. Elated.

                    PATRICK
          Thanks for not calling me "Nothing" by
          the way. It's an endless nightmare. And
          these assholes actually think they're
          being original.

Brad Hays puts on his helmet and rushes onto the field.
Charlie dries his hands on his pants. So nervous. A 5
second silence that feels like a year. Think of something to
say. Anything.

                    CHARLIE
          So, uh... you like football?

                    PATRICK
          Love it.

                    CHARLIE
          Then, maybe you know my broth--

                    PATRICK
          Hey, Sam.

Charlie looks up. Standing there is the prettiest girl he's
ever seen. **SAM** (17) would make every mother proud and every
father nervous. She is alive, adventurous, and a world class
flirt. Great attitude. Great taste. Great banter.

                    SAM
          Question. Could the bathrooms here be
          more disgusting?

                    PATRICK
          Yes, they call it the men's room.

Sam sits down, sandwiching Charlie between her and Patrick.
Charlie tries to remain casual. Hang in there, buddy.

                    SAM
        Well, I finally got hold of Bob.

                    PATRICK
        Party tonight?

                    SAM
        No. He's still trying to shag that
        waitress from the Olive Garden.

                    PATRICK
        He's never tossing that salad.

Brad Hays marches the Devils offense down the field. The
kids clap. Sam looks at Charlie, then turns back to Patrick.

                    SAM
            (about Charlie)
        Patrick... who's this?

                    PATRICK
        This is...

                    CHARLIE
        Uh... Charlie... Kelmeckis.

                    PATRICK
        Kelmeckis! No shit! Your sister dates
        Pony Tail Derek, doesn't she?

                    CHARLIE
        Is that what they call him?

                    SAM
        Awww. Leave Pony Tail Derek alone. You
        put the "ass" in "class," Patrick.

                    PATRICK
        I try, Sam. I try.

                    SAM
        It's nice to meet you, Charlie. I'm Sam.

Sam extends her hand to Charlie. Every nail a different
color. They shake. Then, Sam grabs a nacho. Zoinks!

                    PATRICK
        So, what's the plan, Sam? You want to go
        to Mary Elizabeth's house?

                    SAM
Can't. She got caught watering down her
parent's brandy with iced tea. Let's
just go to Kings.

                    PATRICK
              (turns to Charlie)
Hey... we're going to Kings after the
game if you want to come.

Charlie nods just as Brad Hays tosses a touchdown pass. The
fans go crazy. Especially Patrick. Charlie smiles.

25   INT. KINGS FAMILY RESTAURANT - NIGHT   25

The Devils' faithful cheer as Brad Hays and his guys enter!
The place is packed. Patrick and Sam drink coffee while
Charlie eats his brownie. They're all excited.

                    SAM
Do you have a favorite band?

                    CHARLIE
I think The Smiths are my favorite.

                    SAM
Are you kidding!? I love The Smiths!
The best breakup band ever. What's your
favorite song?

                    CHARLIE
Asleep. It's from Louder Than Bombs. I
heard it on Pony Tail Derek's mix tape.

                    PATRICK
That works on so many levels.

                    CHARLIE
I could make a copy for you.

                    SAM
Thanks. What about Eide's? You love
Eide's, right?

                    CHARLIE
              (never heard of it)
Yeah. They're great.

                    PATRICK
Not a band, Charlie.

                    SAM
It's an old record store downtown.

                    PATRICK
          I used to be popular before Sam got me
          some good music. So, watch out, Charlie.
          She'll ruin your life forever.

                    CHARLIE
          That's okay.

Brad Hays, the quarterback, passes with his posse. Taunting.

                    NOSE TACKLE & LINEBACKER
          Hey, Nothing. Hey, Nothing.

                    PATRICK
          Let it go! Jesus! It's an old joke!
          It's over!

Sam laughs. She loves watching Patrick get riled up.

                    SAM
          So, Charlie... what are you going to do
          when you get out of here?

                    CHARLIE
          My Aunt Helen said I should be a writer,
          but I don't know what I'd write about.

                    SAM
          You could write about us.

                    PATRICK
          Yeah. Call it Slut and The Falcon. Make
          us solve crimes.

Sam laughs. Charlie smiles.

                    CHARLIE
          You guys look happy together. How long
          have you been boyfriend and girlfriend?
               (off their laughs)
          What?

                    SAM
          He's my step-brother. My mom finally
          left my worthless dad and married his
          nice dad 3 years ago.

                    PATRICK
          But Sam's not bitter. Make no mistake.

                    SAM
          Absolutely. I'm not a bulimic. I'm a
          bulim-ist.

They laugh at their inside joke. Charlie has no idea what's
so funny.

>   CHARLIE
>   I'm sorry. I don't know what that means.

>   PATRICK
>   She just really believes in bulimia.

>   SAM
>   (cracking up)
>   I love bulimia.

26   EXT. CHARLIE'S HOUSE - NIGHT   26

Charlie hops out of Sam's old truck.   The music blares.

>   PATRICK
>   Thanks for paying, Charlie.

>   CHARLIE
>   (so eager)
>   No problem. Thanks for the ride. Hey...
>   maybe I'll see you around in school?

>   SAM
>   (distracted - to Patrick)
>   God, would you turn that down? You're
>   going to make us deaf. Bye, Charlie.

>   PATRICK
>   Bye, Charlie.

>   CHARLIE
>   Okay. Bye.

Charlie waves as the truck leaves. The look on his face.
The happiness from one night of company.

27   INT. CHARLIE'S HOUSE - NIGHT   27

Charlie enters the house, excited to tell someone his news.
He runs up the stairs to find the living room empty. He
hears the TV playing downstairs in the basement.

28   INT. DOORWAY TO BASEMENT - NIGHT   28

As Charlie approaches, he hears muffled sounds of <u>fighting</u>.

>   DEREK (O.S.)
>   I'm sorry. I can't do anything about it.
>   Please talk to me.

                    CANDACE (O.S.)
          Maybe your mom and I should have a "drive
          us to our hair appointment" contest.
          Then, I could spend a Saturday with you.

Charlie looks through a slit in the open door to find...

                    DEREK
          There's nothing I can do--

                    CANDACE
          Do you always want to be a mama's boy?

                    DEREK
          I am not a mama's boy--

                    CANDACE
          Yes! You are! Every time I go to your
          house--

                    DEREK
          Shhh. Shut u--

                    CANDACE
          -- your mom says, "Don't go to Columbia
          with Candace. Go to Pitt, Derek. Mommy
          needs you to stay at home because she
          can't drive herself." She's only 51.

                    DEREK
          SHUT UP, CANDACE!

29   INT. CHARLIE'S HOUSE - BASEMENT - CONTINUOUS   29

Charlie enters, wanting to stop the fight. Derek's neck is
red. Dangerous angry. Candace keeps digging.

                    CANDACE
          And you just stand there like a little
          bitch dog.

SNAP! Out of nowhere, Derek slaps her across the face. It's
not a movie slap. It's a real slap. Dead sound. And after
it, silence. Candace turns and sees Charlie. It sobers her
up. Charlie moves at Derek. Candace stops him.

                    CANDACE (CONT'D)
          Charlie, just go. I can handle it. Just
          don't wake up mom and dad.

She pushes him out of the room and closes the door.

30   INT. CHARLIE'S BEDROOM - NIGHT   30

Charlie sits at his desk. So disturbed. He hears a car
start outside. He moves to his window and looks down at
Derek and Candace near Derek's mother's Mercedes. Derek is
crying. Candace comforts. After a beat... they kiss.

Charlie stands frozen, a look creeping across his face.

                    MOTHER (V.O.)
          Hey, look who's here...

                                              FLASHBACK TO:

31   INT. ENTRY HALL - NIGHT (FLASHBACK)   31

The door opens to reveal Charlie's mom and **AUNT HELEN**
entering the house. Aunt Helen carries a suitcase. The
children don't know where she's been or why she looks sad.
They just know they love her. Little Charlie stands at the
top of the stairs with his brother and sister in their Sunday
clothes. There are balloons. And streamers.

                    LITTLE CANDACE
          Welcome home, Aunt Helen!

                    AUNT HELEN
          Oh. Look at you all, dressed so nice.

Aunt Helen smiles at Little Charlie on top of the stairs.

                                              MATCH CUT TO:

32   INT. ENTRY HALL - NIGHT (PRESENT)   32

Charlie stands at the top of the stairs as Candace enters the
house. She is startled when she sees Charlie. They whisper.

                    CHARLIE
          What are you doing?

                    CANDACE
          Look, I egged him on. You saw it. He's
          never hit me before. I promise he'll
          never hit me again.

She's about to go back downstairs when...

                    CHARLIE
          Like Aunt Helen's boyfriends?

A silence passes between them. Then...

                              CANDACE
               Charlie... this is Pony Tail Derek. I
               can handle him. Will you trust me?
               Please, don't tell mom and dad.

With a desperately confident nod, Candace goes downstairs.
Charlie stands in the entry hall, troubled.

33   INT. GYMNASIUM - NIGHT   33

The Homecoming Dance is in full swing. God bless everyone.
Especially Charlie. He's alone at the wall, dressed in his
Sunday suit. To us, adorable. To himself, in living hell.

Charlie watches his sister, slow dancing with Derek. As
happy as she looks, Charlie still isn't sure if he did the
right thing by keeping quiet. The song ends to applause.

After a beat, Charlie turns away. That's when he sees Sam
and Patrick at the punch bowl. We hear the first notes of
"Come On, Eileen" by Dexy's Midnight Runners.

                              SAM
               Oh, my God. They're playing good music.

                            PATRICK
               Holy shit. They are! They're playing
               good music!

                              SAM
                   (total mischief)
               Living room routine?

                            PATRICK
               Living room routine!

Charlie watches Sam and Patrick run to the center of the
floor and show this stiff crowd what dancing is. It starts
slow. "So over it" hand moves. A little shoulder. And
then, the best of swing. 30 seconds of genius.

Charlie takes a breath. Then, he tries desperately not to
look like he's dancing toward them as he dances toward them.
He bobs his head like a dork. And once he gets close,
Patrick and Sam turn and find him.

                         SAM & PATRICK
               Hey!

Without a pause, they grab his hands, and move together in a
circle. Their own island. After a moment, Sam moves around
Charlie like a maypole as the whole gym explodes into dance.

34   EXT. BOB'S HOUSE - NIGHT   34

The party rages inside this mansion in the rich part of town.
Patrick and Sam walk up the steps with Charlie tailing.

                    SAM
          God, it's freezing.

                    PATRICK
          But you wore that toasty costume. It's
          not like you're trying too hard to be
          original.

                    SAM
          Piss off, Tennessee Tuxedo.

                    CHARLIE
          Are you sure it's okay that I come?

                    SAM
          Of course. Just remember, Charlie...
          Bob's not paranoid.

                    PATRICK
          "He's sensitive."

Sam knocks. The door opens, revealing **BOB** (20). Bob was the
cool high school kid, who never quite left. He's stoned so
often that people can't tell the difference anymore.

                    BOB
          Sam... that waitress from the Olive
          Garden is a tease. Will you marry me?

                    SAM
          Only if I have Patrick's blessing.

                    BOB
          Patrick?

                    PATRICK
          You're a hopeless stoner who attends the
          culinary institute. So, I'm going to
          have to say "no" on that one, but nice
          try. Charlie?

Patrick leads Charlie inside, leaving Bob staring at Sam.

                    BOB
          Touché.

35   INT. BOB'S BASEMENT - MOMENTS LATER   35

                    PATRICK
          Charlie... <u>this</u> is a party.

The music blasts. Charlie's eyes are our guide. As they
walk through the crowd, you can smell it. Stale beer and
cigarette smoke. High school parties. The room is packed
with kids playing quarters. Others pouring vodka into a
watermelon.

                    PATRICK (CONT'D)
          This is what fun looks like.

Patrick smiles when he spots two friends.

                    PATRICK (CONT'D)
          You ready to meet some desperate women?

MARY ELIZABETH and ALICE (both 17) sit on the sofa together.
Mary Elizabeth is smart, a little overweight, and extremely
bossy. Alice will figure out that she's a lesbian in
college. Right now, she just likes movies and is Mary
Elizabeth's "beta female."

                    PATRICK (CONT'D)
          Here, have a seat. Hey, ladies, meet
          Charlie. Charlie, meet ladies.

They shake hands and say their hellos.

                    PATRICK (CONT'D)
          This is Charlie's first party ever. So,
          I expect nice, meaningful, heartfelt blow
          jobs from both of you.

                    MARY ELIZABETH
          Patrick, you're such a dick.

                    PATRICK
          Where the hell did you go?

                    MARY ELIZABETH
          The dance was a little boring, don't you
          think?

                    PATRICK
          You're so selfish. We looked everywhere
          for you. You could have told someone.

                    MARY ELIZABETH
          Cry me a river.

                    PATRICK
          How is it that you got meaner since

                    MARY ELIZABETH
          Just lucky I guess.

                    PATRICK
          I think you're doing something wrong.

                    MARY ELIZABETH
          Or something very right.

Patrick and Mary Elizabeth laugh at their banter, just as Sam
calls out from the other side of the room.

                    SAM (O.S.)
          Hey! Look who's here!

The party turns, and Charlie sees <u>Brad Hays</u>, the quarterback,
enter with Sam and Bob. Patrick approaches them. Charlie
sits on the beat up couch next to the girls. He's shocked.

                    CHARLIE
          Is that Brad Hays?

                    ALICE
          Yeah. He comes here sometimes.

                    CHARLIE
          But he's a popular kid.

                    MARY ELIZABETH
             (offended)
          Then, what are <u>we</u>?

Charlie tries to think of something, but he can't. The girls
turn, ignoring him. Bob approaches with a tray.

                    BOB
          Charlie, you look like you could use a
          brownie.

                    CHARLIE
          Thank you. I was so hungry at the dance.
          I was going to go to King's, but I didn't
          really have any time. Thanks.

Bob smiles. Mary Elizabeth gives Alice a knowing glance.
Charlie bites into the brownie. The icing gushing between
his teeth. The image goes up into the smoke like an inhale
as he chews and chews and chews.

36   INT. BOB'S BASEMENT - LATER   36

After a beat, the music changes, and the image exhales back
down to Charlie, who is now... baked out of his mind. The

whole party surrounds him now, pissing themselves with
laughter as this shy kid <u>talks</u> and <u>talks</u> and <u>talks</u>.

                    CHARLIE
          Have you guys felt this carpet? This
          carpet feels so darn good.

                    MARY ELIZABETH
               (laughing)
          Charlie, what do you think about high
          school?

                    CHARLIE
          High school? Bullshit. The cafeteria is
          called the Nutrition Center. And people
          wear their letter jackets even when it's
          98 degrees out. And why do they give out
          letters for marching band? That's not a
          sport, and we all know it.

                    MARY ELIZABETH
          This kid is crazy.

Charlie looks at Mary Elizabeth with her new wave haircut.

                    CHARLIE
          And Mary Elizabeth, I think you're really
          going to regret that haircut when you
          look back at old photographs.
               (off their laughter)
          I'm really sorry. That sounded like a
          compliment in my head.

                    MARY ELIZABETH
          Oh, my God!

                    ALICE
          Well, it's kind of true.

                    MARY ELIZABETH
          Shut up!

Sam enters the room. Takes quick stock. Then...

                    SAM
          Bob, did you get him stoned?

                    BOB
          Come on, Sam. He likes it. Just look at
          him.

                    SAM
          How do you feel, Charlie?

                    CHARLIE
          I just really want a milkshake.

The entire room explodes with laughter. Charlie loves that
people find him so funny.

37   INT. BOB'S KITCHEN - NIGHT   37

Sam takes the ice cream from the freezer to the blender.
Charlie watches her make the perfect vanilla milkshake.

                    CHARLIE
          Sam, you have such pretty brown eyes, the
          kind of pretty that deserves to make a
          big deal about itself. You know what I
          mean?

                    SAM
          Okay, Charlie. Let me make the milkshake.

                    CHARLIE
          What a great word. Milkshake. It's like
          when you say your name over and over
          again in the mirror, and after awhile, it
          sounds crazy.

                    SAM
          I'm guessing you've never been high
          before?

                    CHARLIE
          Me? No. My best friend Michael. His
          dad was a big drinker. So, he hated all
          that stuff. Parties, too.

                    SAM
          Well, where is Michael tonight?

                    CHARLIE
          Oh, he shot himself last May.

Sam looks up. Shocked silent. Charlie is just stoned.

                    CHARLIE (CONT'D)
          I kind of wish he'd left a note. You
          know what I mean?
               (off her sad nod)
          Where's the bathroom?

                    SAM
          It's up the stairs.

                    CHARLIE

Charlie wanders off. Sam watches him go.

38   INT. HALLWAY - NIGHT   38

Charlie leaves the bathroom and stops when he sees himself in
a large ornate mirror in the hallway.

                    CHARLIE
          Charlie. Charlie. Weird.

Charlie wanders down the hallway, a little lost. He finds
the door to the master bedroom and opens it. He sees Patrick
and Brad Hays... <u>kissing</u>.

                    CHARLIE (CONT'D)
          Woah.

                    PATRICK
          Charlie?

                    BRAD HAYS
               (nervous)
          Who is that kid?

                    PATRICK
          Relax. Relax. He's a friend of mine.
          Stay here.

Patrick closes the bedroom door and follows Charlie.

                    CHARLIE
          I didn't see anything.

                    PATRICK
          I know you saw something, but it's okay.

Patrick takes a quick peek to make sure no one is watching.

                    PATRICK (CONT'D)
          Listen, Brad doesn't want anyone to
          know... wait, are you baked?

                    CHARLIE
          "Like a cake." That's what Bob said.
          And how you can't have 3 on a match
          because they would find us. And everyone
          laughed, but I don't know what's funny.

                    PATRICK
          Okay, Charlie, listen. I need you to
          promise that you're not going to say
          anything to anyone about me and Brad.
          This has to be our little secret.

                    CHARLIE
          Our little secret. Agreed.

                    PATRICK
          Thank you. We'll talk later.

                    CHARLIE
          I look forward to that big talk.

Patrick laughs, goes back to the room, and closes the door.

39   INT. BOB'S BASEMENT - NIGHT   39

The party has thinned. Sam watches Charlie drink his
milkshake obsessively with Alice and Mary Elizabeth.

                    CHARLIE
          Isn't this the best milkshake, Alice?
          It's even better than the first one.

Patrick walks downstairs. Sam motions him over.

                    SAM
               (barely audible whisper)
          I need to talk to you. Charlie just told
          me that his best friend shot himself. I
          don't think he has any friends.

Patrick turns to look at Charlie. He feels so bad for the
kid. Patrick raises his plastic cup to the remaining crowd.

                    PATRICK
          Everyone. Raise your glasses to Charlie.

Charlie looks up. A little paranoid. Everyone is staring.

                    CHARLIE
          What did I do?

                    PATRICK
          You didn't do anything. We just want to
          toast our new friend.
               (off his look)
          You see things. And you understand.
          You're a wallflower.

Charlie dries his sweaty hands on his pants. He looks around
the room at the nods and friendly faces.

                    PATRICK (CONT'D)
          What is it? What's wrong?

                    CHARLIE

                    PATRICK
          Well, we didn't think there were any cool
          people left to meet. So, everyone...

                    SAM & EVERYONE
          To Charlie.

They all drink. Sam approaches him. A knowing smile.

                    SAM
          Welcome to the island of misfit toys.

Charlie smiles, and the soundtrack comes rushing up loud.

                                        SMASH CUT TO:

40   EXT./INT. SAM'S TRUCK - NIGHT   40

The truck speeds on Highway 376 toward the Fort Pitt Tunnel.
Patrick drives. Sam cranks the radio, blaring "The Tunnel
Song." The Star's anthem, "Your Ex-Lover is Dead" is our
prototype for tone.

                    SAM
          My God. What is this song!?

                    PATRICK
          Right? I have no idea.

                    SAM
             (to Charlie)
          Have you heard it before?

                    CHARLIE
          Never.

                    SAM
             (light bulb)
          Wait! Let's go through the tunnel!

                    PATRICK
          Sam, it's freezing.

                    SAM
          Patrick, it's the perfect song!

                    PATRICK
          No. Mama Patrick says no.

                    SAM
          Patrick, it's Sam. It's Sam talking to
          you, I'm begging you to drive me--

                    PATRICK
                   (laughing)
              Alright! I concede!

Sam climbs through the window to the flat bed. She grips the
flood lights to steady herself as she stands.

                    CHARLIE
              What is she doing?

                    PATRICK
              Don't worry. She does it all the time.

                    SAM
              Turn it up!

                    PATRICK
              You got it, your highness.

Patrick turns up the volume and drums on the steering wheel,
just as the truck flies into...

THE TUNNEL

We go behind the truck. Rising as Sam puts her arms in the
air. The image moves to Charlie's point of view, rising from
Sam's feet up her shivering legs. Past the band-aid on her
right knee. To Sam's face as she looks down. Into the
camera. Right at us. For we are now...

Charlie, looking up at Sam, so in love with this free-spirit.
So happy to have friends. Happy to be alive. Charlie gets
this look on his face. Patrick notices and smiles.

                    PATRICK (CONT'D)
              What?

                    CHARLIE
              I feel infinite.

The truck flies out of the Fort Pitt Tunnel onto the bridge.
Patrick and Charlie laugh as Sam raises her arms. Free and
young and alive on the greatest night of Charlie's life.

                                             CUT TO:

41 INT. CHARLIE'S BEDROOM - AFTERNOON   41

We see Charlie proudly put a Smiths poster on his wall next
to photos of his new friends. He dances to his desk,
listening to Air Supply's "All Out of Love" on his Walkman.

> CHARLIE (V.O.)
> Dear Friend, I'm sorry I haven't written
> for awhile, but I've been trying hard not
> to be a loser.

As the lyrics begin, Charlie unabashedly lip-synchs...

> AIR SUPPLY
> *I'm lying alone with my head on the*
> *phone, thinking of you 'til it hurts.*

Charlie sits at his desk, writing and lip-synching.

> CHARLIE (V.O.)
> For example, I am trying to participate
> by listening to Sam's collection of big
> rock ballads and thinking about love.
> Sam says they are kitschy and brilliant.
> I completely agree.

42   INT. BILL'S CLASSROOM - MORNING   42

As the students file out, Charlie hands his paper to Bill in
exchange for a beat up copy of The Great Gatsby.

> CHARLIE (V.O.)
> I am also studying extra books outside of
> class. As it turns out, Mr. Anderson is
> a writer. He even had a play put up in
> New York once, which I think is very
> impressive. He and his wife might go
> back there after this year. I know this
> is selfish, but I really hope he doesn't.

Charlie pauses in the doorway and turns back to look at Bill.

43   INT. CAFETERIA - LUNCH   43

Charlie turns from the lunch line with The Great Gatsby on
his tray. He looks at the gang at their table. He sits with
them as they debate the design of this month's fanzine.

> CHARLIE (V.O.)
> My favorite time, though, is lunch because
> I get to see Sam and Patrick. We spend
> the time working on Mary Elizabeth's
> fanzine about music and The Rocky Horror
> Picture Show. It's called Punk Rocky.
> Mary Elizabeth is really interesting
> because she is a Buddhist and a punk, but
> somehow she always acts like my father at
> the end of a "long day."

44   INT. LIBRARY - AFTERNOON   44

The xerox spits out copies of PUNK ROCKY! Halloween Issue!
Alice staples while Mary Elizabeth works her like a sled dog.

                    CHARLIE (V.O.)
          Her best friend Alice loves vampires and
          wants to go to film school. She also
          steals jeans from the mall. I don't know
          why because her family is rich, but I'm
          trying not to be judgemental. Especially
          since I know how they were all there for
          Patrick last year. Patrick never likes
          to be serious, so it took me awhile to
          get what happened.

Sam and Alice laugh when Patrick begins stapling Mary
Elizabeth's fanzines to within an inch of their life.

*[Note: The following sequence will come from Charlie's POV of
Patrick and Brad's activities over a weekend.]*

45   EXT. FOOTBALL STADIUM - NIGHT   45

Brad Hays leads the football team through the banner onto the
field as Charlie, Patrick, and Sam cheer. Moments later,
Brad pulls his helmet on and rushes onto the field.

                    CHARLIE
          When he was a junior, Patrick started
          seeing Brad on the weekends in secret. I
          guess it was hard, too, because Brad had
          to get drunk every time they fooled
          around.

46   INT. CAFETERIA - LUNCH   46

Patrick whispers while the gang studies their SAT books.

                    CHARLIE (V.O.)
          Then, Monday in school, Brad would say,
          "Man, I was so wasted. I don't remember
          a thing." This went on for 7 months.

47   INT. ST. THOMAS MORE CATHOLIC CHURCH - MORNING   47

Charlie sits with his family in itchy church clothes. He
turns to see Brad with his father and mother. Proper family.
Brad's dad gives him a pat on the back.

                    CHARLIE (V.O.)
          When they finally did it, Brad said he
          loved Patrick. Then, he started to cry.

                    CHARLIE (V.O.) (CONT'D)
          saying his dad would kill him. And
          saying he was going to hell.

48   INT. LIBRARY - DAY   48

     We see Patrick and Brad walking in the library. They reach
     the stacks, and just when it looks like they'll speak, they
     simply... PASS EACH OTHER WITHOUT A WORD.

                    CHARLIE (V.O.)
          Patrick was eventually able to help Brad
          get sober. I asked Patrick if he felt
          sad that he had to keep it a secret, and
          he said no because at least now, Brad
          doesn't have to get drunk to love him.

     Brad sits down with his football pals. Patrick joins Charlie
     and Sam at their table. Charlie looks over at Sam, studying
     hard for her SAT's.

                    CHARLIE (CONT'D)
          I think that I understand because I
          really like Sam. I asked my sister about
          her, and she said that when Sam was a
          freshman, the upper classmen used to get
          her drunk at parties. I guess she had a
          reputation. But I don't care. I'd hate
          for her to judge me based on what I used
          to be like.

49   INT. CHARLIE'S BEDROOM - DUSK   49

     We see Charlie making a mix tape on his boom box.

                    CHARLIE (V.O.)
          So, I've been making her a mix tape so
          she will know how I feel.

     The two cassettes run. The song is just about to finish
     when... the side runs out of tape and snaps off.

                    CHARLIE (CONT'D)
          Ah, shit!

50   EXT. DORMONT HOLLYWOOD MOVIE THEATER - MIDNIGHT   50

     The marquee announces it's time for the...

51   INT. DORMONT HOLLYWOOD MOVIE THEATER - MIDNIGHT   51

     ... Rocky Horror Picture Show! The **ROCKY EMCEE**, dressed as
     Riff Raff, whips the crowd into a frenzy.

```
        ROCKY EMCEE                          CROWD
Gimme an R!  Gimme an O!        R-O-C-K-Y!  Rocky!  Rocky!
Gimme a C!  Gimme a K!  Gimme   Rocky!
a Y!  What's that spell!?
```

The crowd cheers! Charlie claps from the front row.

52   INT. DORMONT HOLLYWOOD MOVIE THEATER - LATER   52

The movie is in full swing. Charlie watches Sam as Janet in
the Floor Show. Sam mimics Susan Sarandon perfectly.
Especially the body. She winks at Charlie as "Fanfare/Don't
Dream It" begins and arriving regally as Frank 'n Furter in
full drag is... Patrick.

                    PATRICK
          Whatever happened to Fae Wray? That
          delicate, satin draped frame? As it clung
          to her thigh, how I started to cry 'cause
          I wanted to be dressed just the same.

Patrick is a rock star. He approaches Charlie. Putting his
ass in his face. Charlie is freaked out and laughing!
Especially when he sees Brad, alone in the back, smiling.

                    PATRICK (CONT'D)
          Give yourself over to absolute pleasure.
          Swim the warm waters of sins of the
          flesh. Erotic nightmares beyond any
          measure. And sensual daydreams to
          treasure forever. Can't you just see it?
          Woah oh oh!

Charlie stops laughing when the orgy begins between Patrick,
Mary Elizabeth (as Columbia), **CRAIG** (21), an art student with
a model's body (as Rocky)... and of course... Sam. Charlie
watches Sam until he can't take his lust (or guilt).

53   INT. CRAIG'S LOFT APARTMENT - KITCHEN - NIGHT   53

We hear the chorus of "Don't Dream It, Be It" as Charlie
watches all of the exciting cast members at the after-show
party. Charlie sees a photo of Sam's naked back on the wall
of Craig's loft. Very arty. Very black & white. Charlie's
lust (and guilt) are now at 11. Alice looks at the photo.

                    ALICE
          It's gorgeous, Craig. What did you use?

Craig is impressive to high school kids. He's a little
pretentious. But his art school life. His red wine. His
loft. Wow. Right now, he holds court in the wine line.

                    CRAIG
Color film, but black and white paper for
the printing. My professor gave me an
"A," but for the wrong reasons. Most of
them are idiots. You'll see what I mean
when you get to college. How were your
SAT's by the way?

                    ALICE
          (worried)
1150. I think I'll get into NYU.

                    CRAIG
Yeah, I hope so.

                    MARY ELIZABETH
          (cruel to Alice)
1490. Harvard. Face!

54   INT. CRAIG'S LOFT APARTMENT - MOMENTS LATER   54

Charlie sees Sam alone on the loft steps. She looks a little
down. He hands Sam a plastic cup and sits next to her.

                    CHARLIE
Hey. Are you okay?

                    SAM
Yeah. Yeah. But I got my SAT results
back. Oops.

                    CHARLIE
You can take them again.

                    SAM
Yeah, it's just if I'm going to Penn
State main campus, I have to do much
better. I wish I would have studied
freshman year. I was a bit of a mess.

                    CHARLIE
I'll help you study for the next one.

                    SAM
Will you?

                    CHARLIE
Yeah, of course.

                    SAM
Thanks, Charlie.

Charlie summons his courage. He hands her the mix tape.

                    SAM (CONT'D)
What's this?

                    CHARLIE
Just a mix tape. No big deal. My
parents have a pretty good stereo. It's
all about that night in the tunnel. I
couldn't find that song we were listening
to, but I'm still searching for it, so--

                    SAM
It's okay. These are great. You have
really good taste, Charlie.

                    CHARLIE
Really?

                    SAM
Yeah. Way better than me as a freshman.
I used to listen to the worst top 40.

                    CHARLIE
No.

                    SAM
Yeah, I did. But then I heard this old
song. Pearly Dew Drops Drop. And I
thought someday I would be at a party in
college or something. And I'd look up
and see this person across the room. And
from that moment, I'd know everything was
going to be okay. You know what I mean?

                    CHARLIE
          (devastated in love)
Yeah.

55   INT. CRAIG'S LOFT APARTMENT - LATER   55

The tape revolves in the stereo, playing a beautiful ballad.
Charlie watches Sam sway to his music like a serenade. Like
she is dancing with him. But she isn't. A wider angle
reveals that she is slow dancing with... Craig.

Charlie is 15 year old CRUSHED. No filter. Just feeling.
Patrick, Alice, and Mary Elizabeth watch Sam across the room.

                    ALICE
So, what do you think?

                    PATRICK
I don't know.

              ALICE
I hope it works out. Craig would be a
big step up from her last boyfriend.

          MARY ELIZABETH
No, shit. Who could forget Mr. Car Wash
Loser?

            PATRICK
I just hope she stops playing dumb with
these guys. I keep telling her... don't
make yourself small. You can't save
anybody.

Craig dips a smiling Sam as the song ends. Sam goes into the
kitchen. Craig approaches Charlie. Turns off his mix tape.

            CRAIG
Man, your mix is morbidly sad, kid. How
about something a little more upbeat?

Craig grabs a record from the pile and slaps it down.

          CRAIG (CONT'D)
Sam tells me you want to be a writer.

           CHARLIE
Yeah.

            ALICE
Don't you write poetry, Craig?

            CRAIG
No. Poetry writes me. You know?

Charlie sighs. Craig's upbeat song begins to play. He
dances over to Sam. Charlie's heart breaks as he watches Sam
hug on Craig.

56   INT. MILL GROVE HIGH SCHOOL - HALLWAY - DAY   56

In a mirror image, Candace hugs on Derek near the lockers.
Charlie closes his own locker and moves down the hall.

57   INT. ENGLISH CLASS - MORNING   57

The bell rings. Charlie sets down his On the Road paper.

            BILL
Wow. That was fast. You want another
one?

Charlie nods. Bill smiles and reaches into his desk. He
hands Charlie a copy of A Separate Piece. Charlie takes the
book and starts to walk out, but he turns back.

>   CHARLIE
>   Mr. Anderson... can I ask you something?

>   BILL
>   Yeah.

>   CHARLIE
>   Why do nice people choose the wrong
>   people to date?

>   BILL
>   Are we talking about anyone specific?

Charlie nods. Bill looks straight at him. Not preaching.
Coming from a history of personal experience and pain.

>   BILL (CONT'D)
>   We accept the love we think we deserve.

>   CHARLIE
>   Can we make them know they deserve more?

>   BILL
>   We can try.

Charlie smiles.

58   INT. KINGS FAMILY RESTAURANT - MORNING   58

Charlie waits nervously at a booth. He sees Sam enter. He
fixes his hair, then pretends to read his SAT PREP BOOK.

>   SAM
>   Hey, Charlie.

>   CHARLIE
>   Hey, Sam. I didn't see you come in. You
>   want to work on probabilities and
>   statistics?

Sam nods. They open their books, and a Christmas song
begins. In a quick passage of time, we see them study next
to Halloween decorations. Then, Thanksgiving. And finally,
Christmas decorations.

59   INT. CHARLIE'S HOUSE - NIGHT   59

The song continues. Charlie's mom and sister hang the
Christmas ornaments as Charlie helps his dad find that "one

                        CHARLIE
             Hey, dad. Can I have 30 dollars?

                        FATHER
                   (old joke)
             20 dollars? What do you want 10 dollars
             for?

                        CHARLIE
             Sam is doing secret santa. It's her
             favorite thing in the world. Please.

Charlie's father reaches into his pocket and hands Charlie a
bill. It's a fifty. Dad winks, in a great mood.

                        FATHER
             Have fun.

                        CHARLIE
             Thanks.

60   INT. MILL GROVE HIGH SCHOOL - DAY   60

Lockers are opened by Charlie. Sam. Patrick. Wrapped gifts
are deposited. Mischief smiles. Lockers closed. Everyone
loves getting their presents except Charlie - who got socks.

61   INT. BILL'S CLASSROOM - MORNING   61

Bill hands Charlie a well worn copy of The Catcher in the
Rye. He smiles.

                        BILL
             Charlie... this was my favorite book
             growing up. This is my copy, but I want
             you to have it.

                        CHARLIE
             Thanks.

                        BILL
             Have a great Christmas break.

                        CHARLIE
             You too, Mr. Anderson.

62   INT. SHOP CLASS - DAY   62

Mr. Callahan, the shop teacher, looks at a Sad Sack Girl's
clock. He takes a moment, and then...

                        MR. CALLAHAN
             Terrible stain.

He moves to Charlie's dad's amazing clock. He hands Charlie
an A on a piece of paper.

                    MR. CALLAHAN (CONT'D)
          That's pretty good, Charlie.

Mr. Callahan moves to Patrick's SHITTY WOODEN CLOCK. No
stain. No finish. Lop-sided. The ugliest clock you've ever
seen in your life.

                    MR. CALLAHAN (CONT'D)
          You've got to be kidding me.

                    PATRICK
          If you fail me, you get me next semester.

Mr. Callahan writes a grade and slaps it down.

63   EXT. WEST END OVERLOOK - NIGHT   63

The song continues as Patrick holds up the grade. C minus!
Charlie and Sam cheer as Patrick screams at the top of his
lungs...

                    PATRICK
          Woo! C Minus! It's over! It's over!
          Ladies and gentlemen, I am below average!

                    SAM
          Below average!

Patrick screams at the city in the distance. Below average!

64   INT. DORMONT HOLLYWOOD MOVIE THEATER - GREEN ROOM - NIGHT   64

We move to find Sam, holding her SAT score up to the group.

                    SAM
          Hey, guys. 1210.

Everyone cheers. Sam hugs Charlie.

65   INT. SAM AND PATRICK'S HOUSE - GAMES ROOM - NIGHT   65

Charlie carries Sam on his shoulders past the Christmas Tree.
Sam wears a Santa Hat like a hot elf.

                    SAM
          No more applications! No more SAT's!
          Thank you, Charlie!

They pass Mary Elizabeth as she opens her final present.

>   MARY ELIZABETH
>   Multiple pairs of blue jeans. Wow. This
>   is a really tough one, but I'm going to
>   have to guess... Alice.

Alice smiles. Bob nudges her. Guilty as charged. Mary
Elizabeth pulls one last item out of the gift bag.

>   MARY ELIZABETH (CONT'D)
>   Wait, guys... a receipt! She actually
>   paid!

>   PATRICK
>   Impossible!

>   MARY ELIZABETH
>   I'm so touched.

Alice laughs. Patrick pours everyone brandy. The kids look
ridiculous, but they don't feel ridiculous.

>   CHARLIE
>   Where's Craig?

>   SAM
>   He went home to Connecticut. He'll be
>   back for New Year's Eve.

>   CHARLIE
>   I'm sorry we won't be seeing him tonight.

Sam nods, then turns. Charlie is delighted. No Craig. The
kids settle in the living room in front of the fire.

>   SAM
>   Alright, big brother by 3 weeks. Who's
>   your secret santa?

>   PATRICK
>   I'll tell you, Sam. This one's tough. I
>   have received a harmonica, a magnetic
>   poetry set, a book about Harvey Milk, and
>   a mix with the song "Asleep" on it...
>   twice.

Charlie starts snickering. He can't help himself.

>   PATRICK (CONT'D)
>   I mean, I have no idea. This collection
>   of presents is so gay that I think I must
>   have given them to myself. But despite
>   that distinct possibility, I'm going to
>   have to go with... drum roll... Charlie.

Charlie holds up his hands. Yay! They all cheer.

                    SAM
          Alright, Charlie... it's your turn.

Charlie and Patrick switch places. Charlie stands.

                    CHARLIE
          Okay. Uh, I have received socks, pants,
          a shirt, and a belt. I was ordered to
          wear them all tonight. So, I'm guessing
          my secret santa is Mary Elizabeth.

                    PATRICK
          Huh. Now, why do you say that?

                    CHARLIE
          I don't know. She bosses people around
          sometimes.

The gang cracks up. Mary Elizabeth is pissed.

                    MARY ELIZABETH
          What the hell is wrong with you?

                    CHARLIE
          Sorry.

                    PATRICK
          Well, you'll be surprised to know that
          your secret santa is actually... me.

                    CHARLIE
          You got me clothes? Why?

                    PATRICK
          Because all the great writers used to
          wear great suits. Your last present is
          on a towel rack in the bathroom. Delve
          into our facilities. Emerge a star.

Charlie gives Sam a sack of presents.

                    CHARLIE
          Can you hand these out while I'm gone?

                    MARY ELIZABETH
          Wait a second. There's only secret santa
          presents. There are rules, Charlie.

                    PATRICK
          Mary Elizabeth, why are you trying to eat
          Christmas? Hand them out, Sam.

Sam gives out the presents. The group rips them open. Alice
looks at a book about Martin Scorsese with the inscription...

                    ALICE
          "Alice, I know you'll get into NYU."

Alice turns to Mary Elizabeth who holds up a card with...

                    MARY ELIZABETH
          40 dollars.
                    (reads card)
          "To print Punk Rocky in color next time."

Bob blows soap bubbles into the air. Stoned. Mesmerized.

                    BOB
          He knows me. He really knows me.

Sam looks at her present. An old 45 record of The Beatles
classic "Something" with a card. She reads the card. Holds
it to her chest. Very moved.

                    SAM
          Come on out, Charlie.

They all chime in. "Let's go, young man!" "Charlie!
Charlie!" Charlie opens the door off camera, and we see his
entrance play off their faces. The reverse angle reveals...

Charlie dressed in his suit. Like the best of English mods
in the 60's. For those of you who know the book, this is the
cover. They all clap. It's magic.

                    PATRICK
          Yeah! What a display of man I have ever
          seen!

Sam and Charlie look at each and smile.

66 INT. SAM'S BEDROOM - LATER   66

The door opens. Sam and Charlie walk into the dark room.

                    CHARLIE
          Where are we going?

                    SAM
          It's a surprise.

Sam flips the switch, bathing the room in light. Sam's room
is so cool. A shrine to music. A xerox that says "The
Beatings Will Continue Until Morale Improves." Virgin Mary
icons. Snow globes. Kitsch.

                    CHARLIE
        Is this your room? It's so cool.

                    SAM
        Thanks.

Sam points to a green box with a red ribbon on her desk.

                    CHARLIE
        You got me a present?

                    SAM
        With all that help on my Penn State
        application? Of course I did. Open it.

Charlie lifts up the box to reveal an OLD MANUAL TYPEWRITER.

                    CHARLIE
        I don't know what to say.

                    SAM
        You don't have to say anything.

Sam goes over and types. "Write about us sometime." He
smiles and types back. "I will." They look at each other.
We can hear a lovely ballad playing downstairs.

                    SAM (CONT'D)
        I'm sorry we can't be here for your
        birthday.

                    CHARLIE
        That's okay. I'm just sorry you have to
        go back and visit your dad.

                    SAM
        I'm in such a great mood, I don't think
        even he could ruin it. I feel like I'm
        finally doing good.

                    CHARLIE
        You are.

                    SAM
        Me? What about you? When I met you, you
        were this scared freshman. And look at
        you in that suit. You're like a sexy
        English school boy. I saw Mary Elizabeth
        checking you out.

                    CHARLIE
            (innocent laugh)
        No.

                    SAM
          Innocent. Worst kind of guys. Never see
          you coming. And parents love you. That's
          like... extra danger.

                    CHARLIE
          Well, it hasn't worked so far.

                    SAM
          Come on. You've never had a girlfriend?
          Not even a 2nd grade valentine?

He shakes his head.

                    SAM (CONT'D)
          Have you ever kissed a girl?

                    CHARLIE
          No. What about you?

                    SAM
          Have I ever kissed a girl?

                    CHARLIE
               (laughs)
          No! Your first kiss...

Sam gets this strange look in her eyes. A little haunted.

                    SAM
          My first kiss? I was 11. His name was
          Robert. He would come over to the house
          all the time.

                    CHARLIE
          Was he your first boyfriend?

                    SAM
          He was my dad's boss.

Charlie goes silent.

                    SAM (CONT'D)
          You know Charlie, I used to sleep with
          guys who treated me like shit. And get
          wasted all the time. But now... I feel
          like I have a chance. I could even get
          into a real college.

                    CHARLIE
          It's true. You can do it.

                    SAM

                    CHARLIE
          My Aunt... she had that same thing done
          to her, too. And she turned her life
          around.

                    SAM
          She must have been great.

                    CHARLIE
          She was my favorite person in the
          world... until now.

Sam smiles. She's very moved.

                    SAM
          Charlie, I know that you know I like
          Craig. But I want to forget that for a
          minute. Okay? I just want to make sure
          that the first person who kisses you
          loves you. Okay?

Charlie nods. And with that, Sam leans over and kisses him.
It starts softly, then Sam wraps her thin arms around him.
Holding on for lonely life. When the song crescendos, and
they part, Charlie and Sam look at each other. Finally...

                    SAM (CONT'D)
          I love you, Charlie.

                    CHARLIE
          I love you, too.

67   EXT. SAM AND PATRICK'S HOUSE - NIGHT   67

The porch lights are as golden as Charlie feels right now.
We see the girls wave to each other and hug Sam.

                    GANG
          "Merry Christmas!" "Good luck at your
          dad's!" "See you at New Year's!"

Patrick approaches Charlie in the doorway.

                    CHARLIE
          Have a good time at your mom's.

                    PATRICK
          Thanks. And Charlie... since you were
          born on Christmas Eve, I figure you don't
          get a lot of birthday presents. So, I
          thought you should have my clock. From
          the heart.

                    CHARLIE
          Thank you, Patrick.

Sam gives Charlie one last hug. Patrick and Sam watch their
friends leave.

                    PATRICK
          I love you guys!

68 EXT. DOWNTOWN PITTSBURGH - NIGHT   68

We fly as high as Charlie feels. Above the city on Christmas
Eve.

69 INT. CHARLIE'S HOUSE - NIGHT   69

The front door opens, revealing Charlie's dad.

                    FATHER
          Hey! Look who's here!

He moves out of the way, and standing there is Charlie's
older brother, **CHRIS KELMECKIS** (19). Chris is handsome,
charismatic, and an all around winner.

                    CHRIS
          Come here, little sister.

                    CANDACE
          Hey, Chris.

Big hug. Chris smiles big and "son flirts" with his mom.

                    CHRIS
          Ma, you look so thin!

                    MOTHER
          10 pounds... Weight Watchers.

Big kiss. When he lets go, he sees Charlie and smiles.

                    CHRIS
          Charlie...

Chris and Charlie look at each other in silence. Then, hug.
As the family moves into the dining room to celebrate, Chris
gives him a quiet...

                    CHRIS (CONT'D)
          Happy birthday.

70 INT. CHARLIE'S DINING ROOM - MOMENTS LATER   70

>   MOTHER
>   Make a wish, honey.

We move closer to Charlie as he makes his wish and blows out
his 16 candles.

                                             MATCH CUT TO:

71   EXT. CHARLIE'S STREET - NIGHT (PRESENT)   71

The wind blows out a candle in one of the luminaria bags.
The suburb is quiet. Not a creature is stirring. Except...

Charlie. He fills a brown paper bag with sand and a candle.
He lights the candle, making the bag glow like a beautiful
lantern. He looks down his street, where families are out
with their kids, doing the same luminaria ritual.

                                             MATCH CUT TO:

72   EXT. CHARLIE'S STREET - NIGHT (FLASHBACK)   72

The same street. Christmas Eve. Many years ago. Aunt Helen
and the kids finish their luminaria bags. Aunt Helen lights
up the candles. They glow.

>   AUNT HELEN
>   Can you see it, Charlie? The luminaria
>   is a landing strip for Santa Claus.

The image goes wide. All of these bags glowing. Beautiful.
Aunt Helen rattles her keys. Whispers.

>   AUNT HELEN (CONT'D)
>   Keep an eye out for him with your brother
>   and sister. I'll be right back.

She bends down and whispers into his ear.

>   AUNT HELEN (CONT'D)
>   I'm going to get your birthday present.

She musses his hair and gets in the car.

                                             END FLASHBACK

73   EXT. CHARLIE'S STREET - NIGHT (PRESENT)   73

Charlie hovers over the glowing luminaria. Something is
bothering him. He shakes it off.

74   INT. CHARLIE'S HOUSE - KITCHEN/DINING ROOM - NIGHT   74

Charlie wanders through the quiet house. He turns the corner
where he finds Chris sitting at the table. He's lit by a
couple of candles and the blinking lights of the Christmas
Tree. He's surrounded by leftovers. Charlie sits.

                    CHARLIE
          Hey.

Chris chews and swallows. Famished. They both whisper.

                    CHRIS
          Hey. God, I missed mom's cooking. You
          have no idea how good you have it. I'm
          actually beginning to hate pizza.

Charlie smiles. Grabs a Hershey Kiss cookie.

                    CHARLIE
          How are you liking school?

                    CHRIS
          Not bad. I'm no brainiac like you or
          Candace. But I'm doing okay.

                    CHARLIE
          Okay? You're playing in a Bowl Game.

Chris laughs. Charlie smiles. A moment passes. Chris
changes his tone. Cautious.

                    CHRIS
          How are you feeling, Charlie?

                    CHARLIE
          Good.

                    CHRIS
          You know what I mean. Is it bad tonight?

                    CHARLIE
          No.

                    CHRIS
          No?

                    CHARLIE
          I'm not picturing things anymore. And
          when I do, I can just shut it off.

                    CHRIS
              (relieved)

48.

                         CHRIS (CONT'D)
          now. And maybe if it does get bad again,
          you can just talk to them, yeah?

                         CHARLIE
          Yeah. Especially Sam. I'm going to ask
          her out at New Years. I think the time
          is right now.

Chris smiles at his kid brother. We hear the church organ.

75   INT. ST. THOMAS MORE CHURCH - MORNING   75

The family moves down the line to receive Holy Communion at
Christmas Mass. Charlie's father, then mother, then sister,
take the sacrament. Charlie is next. The PRIEST makes the
motion of the cross with the communion wafer. He places it
in Charlie's hand. Charlie brings the sacrament to his mouth
with his fingers...

                                             MATCH CUT TO:

76   INT. BOB'S LIVING ROOM - NIGHT   76

We move in closer to Charlie's fingers in his mouth. When he
takes his hand out, we see... a tab of LSD. The church organ
is now a rock organ. And it's now... New Year's Eve.

Charlie closes his mouth. He looks down the hall of the
smoky room where Craig has his arm around Sam. Charlie turns
to Mary Elizabeth, who's also dosed.

                         CHARLIE
          How long does this take to work?

77   EXT. BOB'S HOUSE - NIGHT   77

About 45 minutes. The sound is muted thick. Slight echoes.
Charlie shovels the snow. Crunch. Fascinated by his breath
making fog. Sam comes outside. She's worried about him.

                         SAM
          Shoveling snow, huh?

                         CHARLIE
          I have to get this driveway clean. Then,
          I have to congratulate you for being
          happy because you deserve it.

                         SAM
          You said that an hour ago.

                         CHARLIE
          Was that tonight? God. I was looking at
          this tree, but it was a dragon, and then

                         SAM
          Okay, Charlie. Don't freak out. Just
          give me the shovel. Calm down. Look up.

She points. Charlie looks up. Sees the stars.

                         SAM (CONT'D)
          Isn't it quiet?

                         CHARLIE
          Sam, you ever think that if people knew
          how crazy you really were, no one would
          ever talk to you?

                         SAM
          All the time. So, you want to put on
          these glasses? They'll protect you.

Sam puts her arm around his shoulder. Protecting him.
Charlie looks through the glasses. The sky bends like a
globe. When he breathes, the sky ripples.

78   INT. BOB'S HOUSE - NIGHT   78

Charlie wanders through the party, tripping out of his mind.
He sits down on the sofa. The world unbends as Charlie takes
off the glasses. Kids walk around the party, leaving ghosts
of themselves behind.

Charlie looks upstairs to find... Sam and Craig kissing.
Craig leads her to the bedroom.

Charlie looks back at the party as kids gather for the New
Years countdown. Patrick leads the charge.

                         PATRICK
              10-9-8...

79   EXT. CHARLIE'S STREET - NIGHT (FLASHBACK)   79

In a QUICK FLASH, we see 7 year old Charlie with Aunt Helen
on Christmas Eve. She bends to whisper in his ear.

                         AUNT HELEN
          It'll be our little secret, all right?

80   INT. BOB'S HOUSE - NIGHT (PRESENT)   80

We are BACK TO PRESENT as Charlie takes a deep breath and
tries to remember that he's at a New Year's party.

                         PATRICK
              7-6-5-4-3-2-1. Happy New Year!

The crowd cheers, leaving ghosts of themselves. Charlie gets
up from the sofa and walks out of Bob's house.

81   EXT. CHARLIE'S STREET - NIGHT   81

Charlie walks down the road under a streetlight. Silhouette.
The road is icy. Charlie lays down and starts moving his
arms in the snow. The memories begin to haunt him.

82   EXT. CHARLIE'S STREET - NIGHT (FLASHBACK)   82

7 year old Charlie waves goodbye to Aunt Helen as she drives
away through the landing strip for Santa Claus.

83   EXT. CHARLIE'S STREET - NIGHT (PRESENT)   83

16 year old Charlie blinks. The memories come faster.

84   INT. AUNT HELEN'S CAR - NIGHT (FLASHBACK)   84

Aunt Helen drives past a tall snow drift. She looks down at
the 45 of The Beatles in the seat next to her. She smiles at
Charlie's birthday present. Then, she looks up as the
headlights of the semi truck smash the windows with a CRASH!

85   INT. CHARLIE'S HOUSE - NIGHT (FLASHBACK)   85

Charlie's mother opens the door, revealing a POLICEMAN. He
turns to Charlie in his party hat. 7 years old and confused.

86   EXT. CHARLIE'S STREET - NIGHT (PRESENT)   86

16 year old Charlie lays on the snow, shivering, as the image
goes high above to reveal he's made a snow angel.

87   INT. HOSPITAL ROOM - AFTERNOON   87

The Emergency room is bustling on New Year's Day. Charlie
looks up as the POLICE, DOCTORS, and his PARENTS tower over
him. He is terrified and does what any kid would do. He
lies his ass off.

                    POLICEMAN
          Did your older friends pressure you?

                    CHARLIE
          No one pressured me into anything. I
          would never do drugs, officer. Never.

                    POLICEMAN
          Then, how did you happen to be passed out
          on the ground at 6 in the morning?

>   CHARLIE
>   Well, um... I was really tired, and uh...
>   I was feeling feverish. So, I went
>   outside for a walk, just to get some cold
>   air. And I started seeing things. So, I
>   passed out.

He waits to see if this worked. And then, unexpectedly...

>   MOTHER
>   (worried)
>   You're seeing things again, Charlie?

>   CHARLIE
>   (oops)
>   Not, uh... Not really.

88   EXT. MILL GROVE HIGH SCHOOL - PARKING LOT - MORNING   88

The tires squish the grey slush puddle as the busses pull
into the dreary parking lot. School is back in session.

89   INT. HALLWAY - MORNING   89

Charlie shakes off the cold, then takes off his overcoat to
reveal... he's wearing his suit from Secret Santa. All the
kids stare. Charlie realizes he made a terrible mistake.

>   CHARLIE
>   It was a Christmas present.

90   INT. BILL'S CLASSROOM - MORNING   90

Charlie sits as Bill hands out the book for the semester...
The Great Gatsby. As the kids chatter, Bill gives Charlie
his own book to start the year... The Stranger.

>   CHARLIE
>   Did you have fun on your break?

>   BILL
>   More fun than you're going to have today,
>   Sinatra.

Bill pats his shoulder and moves on. The Smart Ass Freshman
looks at Charlie and whispers.

>   SMART ASS FRESHMAN
>   Nice look, jag off.

91   EXT. DORMONT HOLLYWOOD MOVIE THEATER - NIGHT   91

The Rocky Horror faithful enter the theater.

                              SAM (O.S.)
                    I called him 30 times.

92   INT. DORMONT HOLLYWOOD MOVIE THEATER - GREEN ROOM - NIGHT   92

Mary Elizabeth and the kids get ready for the floor show.

                        MARY ELIZABETH
               Well what are we supposed to do? We're
               going on in 10 minutes!

The phone rings. Mary Elizabeth picks up. Charlie turns to
Brad, sitting next to him. Charlie is freaking out.

                          CHARLIE
               But they said in health class--

                         BRAD HAYS
               They say that about LSD to scare you.

                          CHARLIE
               Are you sure?

                         BRAD HAYS
               Charlie, you're fine, man.

Mary Elizabeth hangs up the phone, frustrated.

                        MARY ELIZABETH
               Guys, we have an emergency. Craig flaked
               out on us again. I need a Rocky. Brad?

                         BRAD HAYS
                     (scared)
               No way. There are people out here.

The group is deflated. They all start thinking. After a
beat, Mary Elizabeth looks at Charlie.

                        MARY ELIZABETH
               Charlie... take off your clothes.

93   INT. DORMONT HOLLYWOOD MOVIE THEATER - LATER   93

You know those dreams you have when you are standing in front
of 200 people in your underwear? Well, this is no dream.

We hear a heart beat as Charlie dances out of the Rocky gauze
and finds himself standing in tight gold underwear, looking
out at 200 people, cheering him on.

His friends can't stop smiling. Especially Mary Elizabeth,
who watches Charlie's little butt in the gold undies. She

94   INT. DORMONT HOLLYWOOD MOVIE THEATER - LATER   94

"Touch-A, Touch-A, Touch Me" is in full swing. Sam slinks
over to Charlie dressed in her white bra and slip.

>   SAM
>   (as Janet)
>   *So if anything grows while you pose.*
>   *I'll oil you up and drop you down. And*
>   *that's just one small fraction of the*
>   *main attraction. You need a friendly*
>   *hand. And I need action!*

Sam grabs Charlie's hands and rubs them all over her chest.

>   *SAM (CONT'D)*
>   *Ah! Touch a touch a touch me! I wanna*
>   *be dirty! Thrill me. Chill me. Fulfill*
>   *me! Creature of the night!*

The song continues. We see flashes of the night's
performance as Charlie goes from train wreck to triumph.
Charlie joins Sam in the kick line, and it feels like it's
just the two of them. On the final beat, Sam gasps...

>   SAM (CONT'D)
>   *Creature of the night!*

The song ends. The cast bows. Sam and Patrick push Charlie
in front for his own curtain call. Everyone cheers. It's
the night he'll never forget.

95   EXT. DORMONT HOLLYWOOD MOVIE THEATER - NIGHT   95

The wind whips. That bracing February cold. Charlie helps
Mary Elizabeth carry the costumes outside to her car.

>   CHARLIE
>   Maybe I could join the cast as an
>   alternate or something?

>   MARY ELIZABETH
>   We're filled up now, but they'll need
>   people after we leave for college. I
>   could put in a good word for you.

>   CHARLIE
>   That'd be great. Thanks.

They put the box in her trunk. Snap it closed. We can't
help but notice the "Keep Your Laws Off My Body" bumper
sticker as Mary Elizabeth tries her best to flirt.

                    MARY ELIZABETH
          Charlie... have you heard of the Sadie
          Hawkins dance?

                    CHARLIE
          The one where the girl asks the guy.

                    MARY ELIZABETH
          Yeah. Well, obviously, it's completely
          stupid and sexist. It's like, "Hey,
          thanks for the crumb." And normally, I'd
          just blow it off because school dances
          suck torture. But, you know, it's my
          last year, and... would you maybe want to
          go with me?

                    CHARLIE
          You want to go with me?

                    MARY ELIZABETH
          I'm sick of macho guys. And you looked
          really cute in your costume. So, what do
          you say?

     Charlie thinks and thinks and...

96   INT. CHARLIE'S HOUSE - DUSK   96

     Ding dong. Charlie's mom opens the door for MARY ELIZABETH.
     Charlie straightens out his church suit. So nervous.

                    MOTHER
          You must be Mary Elizabeth. It's so good
          to meet you.

                    MARY ELIZABETH
          You, too, Mrs. Kelmeckis.

                    FATHER
               (shit eating grin)
          Charlie tells me you're a Buddhist.

97   INT. CHARLIE'S HOUSE - FIREPLACE - DUSK   97

     Charlie and Mary Elizabeth stand next to Candace and Derek.

                    FATHER
          OK, a little closer together. That looks
          nice. Buddhist, I need you to smile a
          little bit more. There you go. Nice.

     Cheese! White flash. The picture of 4 kids. Smiling big.

98   INT. MILL GROVE HIGH SCHOOL - GYMNASIUM - NIGHT   98

Charlie and Mary Elizabeth slow dance to an 80's love song.
Sweaty palms. Awkward. Hands on hips. Horror.

Charlie looks around the gym. He sees Alice dancing with her
date, an EFFEMINATE GOTH KID (17). We'll never meet him, but
he'll make us laugh once.

Charlie then watches Patrick dance with Sam. He follows
Patrick's gaze across the floor to Brad, who dances with a
SENIOR GIRL (18). Charlie sees the boys look at each other.
For one moment, it's like they're dancing together.

99   INT. MILL GROVE HIGH SCHOOL - GYMNASIUM - LATER   99

Mary Elizabeth is at the punch bowl with the gang. Charlie
sees Sam, standing by the wall, looking sad. He approaches.

                    CHARLIE
          Are you having a good time?

                    SAM
          Not really. How about you?

                    CHARLIE
          I don't know. This is my first date, so
          I don't know what to compare it to.

                    SAM
          Don't worry. You're doing fine.

Charlie joins her at the wall. Mary Elizabeth gives them a
quick, jealous look.

                    CHARLIE
          I'm sorry Craig didn't come.

                    SAM
          Yeah. He said he didn't want to go to
          some stupid high school dance. Can't say
          I blame him.

                    CHARLIE
          I don't know. If you like it, he should
          come.

                    SAM
          Thanks, Charlie. Have a beautiful first
          date. You deserve it.

                    CHARLIE
          I'll try not to make you too jealous.

He said it to cheer her up. Sam forces a smile and leaves.

100   INT. MARY ELIZABETH'S DEN/LIVING ROOM - NIGHT   100

Mary Elizabeth approaches Charlie on the antique sofa. She
uncorks a bottle of wine. POP! She hands him the bottle.

                    MARY ELIZABETH
          Mmmm. Now, let it breathe.

Mary Elizabeth walks over to the vintage turntable. She
turns on the gas fireplace with a remote control. Roar!

                    CHARLIE
          This is sure a nice house.

                    MARY ELIZABETH
          Thanks.

Mary Elizabeth drops the needle on a vinyl LP. A Doo Wop
make-out classic begins to play. She dances over to Charlie.

                    MARY ELIZABETH (CONT'D)
          Mmmm. Don't you just love old music?
              (off his nod)
          Good. Because I made you a mix of it.
          I'd love to expose you to great things.
          Like Billie Holiday and foreign films.

She pours the wine. Charlie looks at the bottle.

                    CHARLIE
          This merlot is really fancy.

                    MARY ELIZABETH
          Yeah. My dad collects wine, but he
          doesn't drink. That's weird, isn't it?

                    CHARLIE
          I guess. Where are your parents?

                    MARY ELIZABETH
          Their club is hosting a cotillion or
          something racist. They'll be gone all
          night.

Mary Elizabeth drops her necklace with a thud. Charlie looks
around. Heart beating.

                    CHARLIE
          That's sure a nice fire.

                    MARY ELIZABETH
          Yeah. After I'm done being a lobbyist, I
          want to move to a house like this in Cape
          Cod. That sounds nice, doesn't it?

                    CHARLIE
          Yeah.

She reaches out and touches his chest.

                    MARY ELIZABETH
          Your heart is beating really fast.

                    CHARLIE
          Is it?

                    MARY ELIZABETH
          Here, feel.

She puts her hand on his. Moves it to his chest.

                    MARY ELIZABETH (CONT'D)
          Charlie?

                    CHARLIE
          Uh-huh?

                    MARY ELIZABETH
          Do you like me?

                    CHARLIE
          Uh-huh.

                    MARY ELIZABETH
          You know what I mean.

                    CHARLIE
          I think so.

                    MARY ELIZABETH
          Don't be nervous.

She slowly moves his hand to her dress strap. It falls off
her shoulder. She leans in for a red wine kiss. She guides
his hand over her bra. He feels her breast. Wow.

                                        MATCH CUT TO:

101 INT. MARY ELIZABETH'S BASEMENT - FANTASY   101

For a quick moment, Charlie imagines he is kissing Sam.
Broken by...

102   INT. MARY ELIZABETH'S BASEMENT - MOMENTS LATER   102

Mary Elizabeth moves his hand away. Charlie blinks, taking a
moment to realize Sam's not the one in the room. The song is
over. The needle turns at the end of the record.

                    MARY ELIZABETH
          Charlie...

She gives him one last kiss. Content, she lays down on his
lap. Peaceful.

                    MARY ELIZABETH (CONT'D)
          I didn't know how it was going to go
          tonight, but it was really nice, huh?

                    CHARLIE
          Yeah.

                    MARY ELIZABETH
          I can't believe it. You of all people.
          I just can't believe you're my boyfriend.

We land on Charlie's face. "What?" And then, we hear the
GARAGE DOOR OPEN.

                    MARY ELIZABETH (CONT'D)
          Oh, shit! My parents!

The mad scramble for clothes begins.

                                             CUT TO:

103   EXT. CHARLIE'S HOUSE - NIGHT   103

Mary Elizabeth's car pulls in front of Charlie's house.
Charlie gets out. Wanting to say he's not her boyfriend.
Not knowing how. Mary Elizabeth smiles. Smitten.

                    MARY ELIZABETH
          See you Monday.

With that, she backs out of the driveway. We see him from
the back of her car, getting smaller and smaller. His
stomach already filling with acid.

                    CHARLIE (V.O.)
          Dear Friend... I'm sorry I haven't
          written for awhile, but things are a
          total disaster.

104   INT. CAFETERIA - LUNCH   104

Sam, Patrick, and Alice are seated around the table. Mary
Elizabeth has her arms around Charlie. Smothering him.

                    MARY ELIZABETH
          We're literally making out, and I'm in my
          bra. Hello! And the front door opens.
          It's my parents! I'm scrambling to get
          my dress on. It was crazy. Right, babe?

Charlie nods, tortured.

                    CHARLIE (V.O.)
          I probably should have been honest about
          how I didn't want to go out with Mary
          Elizabeth after Sadie's, but I really
          didn't want to hurt her feelings.

105   EXT. MILL GROVE HIGH SCHOOL PARKING LOT - MORNING   105

Ash Wednesday. Charlie gets out of the school bus to
immediately find Mary Elizabeth waiting for him. She sees
the cross of ashes on his forehead. She thinks his ashes are
a smudge. She cleans it.

                    CHARLIE (V.O.)
          You see, Mary Elizabeth is a really nice
          person underneath the part of her that
          hates everyone. And since I heard that
          having a girlfriend makes you happy, I
          tried hard to love her like I love Sam.

                    MARY ELIZABETH
          Can you believe it's almost our two week
          anniversary?

                    CHARLIE
          I know.

106   EXT. DORMONT HOLLYWOOD MOVIE THEATER - NIGHT   106

A double date. Craig and Sam buy the tickets to see the
silent classic, The Cabinet of Dr. Caligari.

                    CHARLIE (V.O.)
          So, I took her on double dates.

                    MARY ELIZABETH
                    (proud)
          Your first foreign film.

                    CHARLIE

                    MARY ELIZABETH
          Vegans don't eat butter.

Charlie tries not to feel Mary Elizabeth's sweaty hand.

                    CHARLIE (V.O.)
          And I tried not to mind that she loves to
          hold hands even when her hands are
          sweaty.

107   INT. MARY ELIZABETH'S DEN/LIVING ROOM - NIGHT   107

Just like Sadie's except... the fire in the fireplace is out.
We move from the fireplace to Charlie, touching Mary
Elizabeth's breasts over her sweater.

                    CHARLIE (V.O.)
          And I had to admit something really
          upsetting. But I am tired of touching
          her boobs. I thought maybe if she would
          just let me pick the make-out music once
          in awhile, we might have a chance.

Charlie looks at the Ani DiFranco Mix on the stereo. Sighs.

108   INT. CAFETERIA - LUNCH   108

The gang is there. Walden rests on Charlie's lunch tray.

                    CHARLIE (V.O.)
          And maybe if she didn't put down the
          books that Mr. Anderson gives me.

                    MARY ELIZABETH
          Walden? I read it in 7th grade. I would
          have called it "On Boring Pond."

109   INT. CHARLIE'S BEDROOM - AFTERNOON   109

Ring! Charlie grabs the cordless. He looks at Patrick's
clock. 3:13pm. His voice can no longer hide his quiet rage.

                    CHARLIE (V.O.)
          Or if she would stop calling me the
          minute I get home from school when I have
          absolutely nothing to talk about other
          than the bus ride home...

                    MARY ELIZABETH (V.O.)
          That dairy just sits with you. It walks
          with you.

Charlie calmly puts down the phone and leaves the room. We

110   INT. CHARLIE'S KITCHEN - MOMENTS LATER   110

Charlie is so miserable. His mom is sympathetic.

                    MOTHER
          She's on the phone right now? Charlie,
          you have to break up with her.

                    CHARLIE
          I can do that?

Charlie's father leans back from the sofa and his newspaper.

                    FATHER
          For Christ's sake... I need to use the
          phone!

111   INT. CHARLIE'S BEDROOM - MOMENTS LATER   111

He returns. Mary Elizabeth is still talking on the cordless.

                    MARY ELIZABETH (V.O.)
          I'll give you this book. It's really how
          I became a vegan--

                    CHARLIE (V.O.)
          I know I should have been honest, but I
          was getting so mad, it was starting to
          scare me.

He looks back at the clock. 3:23pm.

                    CHARLIE (CONT'D)
          Um... Mary Elizabeth. Can I talk to you--

                    MARY ELIZABETH (V.O.)
          Charlie. Please, don't interrupt. You
          know I hate that.

Charlie goes to his quiet place. Tick. Tick. Tick.

                    CHARLIE (V.O.)
          I just wish I could have found another
          way to break up. In hindsight, I
          probably could not have picked a worse
          way to be honest with Mary Elizabeth.

112   INT. CRAIG'S LOFT APARTMENT - NIGHT   112

Truth or dare. The gang is seated in a circle, drinking from
plastic cups. Charlie sits between Mary Elizabeth and Sam.

                        BOB

                    PATRICK
         Who are you talking to?

                    BOB
         I dare you to kiss Alice.

                    PATRICK
              (licks his lips)
         Get ready, breeder.

As Patrick approaches an apprehensive Alice...

                    CRAIG
         Mary Elizabeth? Samantha told me that
         you got into Harvard. Congratulations.

                    MARY ELIZABETH
         Thank you.
              (re: Charlie)
         This one still hasn't gotten me flowers.
              (to Charlie)
         But I forgive you.

She kisses him. Charlie bites his cheeks. Sam looks a
little depressed.

                    CRAIG
              (to Sam)
         Don't worry about Penn State. You're
         just wait-listed.

                    PATRICK
         Excuse me, everyone, but you're missing
         some hot "fag on goth" action.

Anticipation. Patrick is getting ready to plant the biggest
kiss on Alice when she jumps him. Everyone groans. Ew!
Laughter. Patrick looks for the next person. Charlie's
heart pounds. Don't pick me! Please!

                    PATRICK (CONT'D)
         Okay. My turn. Um... let's think...
         Charlie... truth or dare?

Silence. Thinking. Finally...

                    CHARLIE
         Truth.

                    PATRICK
         How is your first relationship going?

                    CHARLIE
        It's so bad that I keep fantasizing that
        one of us is dying of cancer, so I don't
        have to break up with her.

                    PATRICK
        Charlie? Truth or dare?

Charlie blinks. It was all fantasy.

                    CHARLIE
        Dare.

                    PATRICK
        I dare you to kiss the prettiest girl in
        the room on the lips. Notice I
        charitably said girl and not person
        because let's face it... I'd smoke all
        you bitches.

Alice hits him. Laughter. Charlie thinks. He looks at Mary
Elizabeth, then turns to Sam. Before Sam can even react...
Charlie plants a kiss right on her lips. When he opens his
eyes, he looks around, and realizes the magnitude of his
mistake. Everyone stares. After a horrible silence...

                    PATRICK (CONT'D)
        Now that's fucked up.

Without a word, Mary Elizabeth just stands, dignified, and
goes into the kitchen.

                    CHARLIE
        Mary Elizabeth, I'm sorry. I'm--

Alice follows Mary Elizabeth. Sam is close behind.

                    CHARLIE (CONT'D)
        Sam?! Sam! I'm sorry. I didn't mean
        anything by it. I'm sorry.

Sam turns and looks at him. She doesn't even recognize him.

                    SAM
        What the hell is wrong with you?

Charlie is devastated.

113   EXT. BOB'S HOUSE - NIGHT   113

They move to the driveway. Charlie feels awful. Panicky.

                    CHARLIE

                    PATRICK
        Trust me. You don't want to go back
        there.

                    CHARLIE
        But, I... I'm sorry... I didn't mean to
        do anything.

                    PATRICK
        I know you didn't, but look... I hate to
        be the one to break this, but there's
        history with Mary Elizabeth and Sam.
        Other guys. Things that have nothing to
        do with you. But... it's best if you
        stay away for awhile.

                    CHARLIE
              (crushed)
        Oh. Okay. How long do you think?

Silence. Charlie looks over at Patrick, who wears a grave
expression. It's going to be a long time. We hear the sound
of the typewriter.

114   INT. CHARLIE'S BEDROOM - MORNING   114

Charlie sits at his desk. It looks like he's barely slept.
He begins typing. The keys up close and loud. Clak.

CLOSE UP TYPING: "Dear friend, I have not seen my friends for
2 weeks now. I am starting to get bad again."

Charlie stares at the typewriter. And remembers.

                                        SMASH CUT TO:

115   INT. CHARLIE'S KITCHEN - NIGHT (FLASHBACK)   115

Little Charlie pops his head around the corner from the
hallway. He looks at something we can't see yet.

                                        BACK TO:

116   INT. CHARLIE'S BEDROOM - MORNING (PRESENT)   116

Present. Knock. Knock. Charlie's mom opens the door.

                    MOTHER
        We're going to be late for Easter Mass.

                    CHARLIE
        I'll... I'll be there in a minute.

Charlie forces a smile, then looks back at the typewriter.
And tries to shake off the memory.

                                        SMASH CUT TO:

117   INT. CHARLIE'S KITCHEN - NIGHT (FLASHBACK)   117

Little Charlie looks at Aunt Helen as she smokes her
cigarette and sobs.

                                        BACK TO:

118   INT. ST. THOMAS MORE CHURCH - MORNING   118

Charlie is lost. His family sits in the pews for Easter
Mass. Charlie watches the PRIEST recite the Lord's prayer.

                    PRIEST
          Our Father who art in Heaven. Hallowed
          be Thy name. Thy kingdom come--

                                        MATCH CUT TO:

119   INT. ST. THOMAS MORE CHURCH - MORNING (FLASHBACK)   119

7 year old Charlie watches the PRIEST recite the Lord's
prayer. He looks at Aunt Helen's picture on the coffin.

                    PRIEST
          Thy will be done on earth as it is in
          Heaven. Give us this day our daily bread.

                                        MATCH CUT TO:

120   INT. ST. THOMAS MORE CHURCH - MORNING (PRESENT)   120

16 year old Charlie looks haunted by the memory.

                    PRIEST
          And forgive us our trespasses as we
          forgive those who trespass against us--

The voices drift away and all Charlie can see is...

                                        CUT TO:

121   INT. CHARLIE'S KITCHEN - NIGHT (FLASHBACK)   121

7 year old Charlie takes Aunt Helen's hand to make her stop
crying.

                                        CUT TO:

122   INT. ST. THOMAS MORE CHURCH - MORNING (PRESENT)   122

16 year old Charlie blinks as the voices come back.

                    PRIEST
          And lead us not into temptation. But
          deliver us from--

                                        SMASH CUT TO:

123   INT. CHARLIE'S BEDROOM - NIGHT   123

Charlie on the phone. His voice wavers a bit. Desperate.

                    CHARLIE (V.O.)
          Mary Elizabeth... I... uh... I've been
          listening to the Billie Holiday CD every
          night and--

                    MARY ELIZABETH (V.O.)
          It's too late, Charlie.

                    CHARLIE
          I know. I just feel really bad about
          what I did. I just get so messed up
          inside like I'm - not there or something.

                    MARY ELIZABETH (V.O.)
          Tell it to someone who cares.

                    CHARLIE
          I know. I'm sorry. I just. We've all
          become such good friends--

                    MARY ELIZABETH (V.O.)
          Good friends? You mean the people I've
          known since kindergarten that you've
          known for 6 months? Those good friends?

                    CHARLIE
          Oh. Yeah. I mean I don't want to do
          anything to ruin our--

                    MARY ELIZABETH (V.O.)
          It's ruined. Okay? So, stop calling
          everyone. Stop embarrassing yourself.

                    CHARLIE
          Okay. I will. Goodbye, Mar--

Dial tone. Charlie hangs up the phone.

124   INT. BOB'S BASEMENT - NIGHT   124

        Charlie is terribly anxious. He watches Bob groom some pot.

                          CHARLIE
                Something's wrong with me--

                          BOB
                Don't worry about it. Hey... you hear
                from Patrick?

                          CHARLIE
                No. He told me to stay away.

                          BOB
                Oh... you don't know?

                          CHARLIE
                    (concerned)
                Why? Why? What happened?

                          BOB
                Brad's father caught them together.

125   INT. MILL GROVE HIGH SCHOOL - HALLWAY - MORNING   125

        As kids open lockers and move to morning period, Charlie
        stares at Brad. He has a black eye and cuts on his face. He
        look like he was beaten up badly. Students whisper gossip.

                          GOSSIP WHISPERS (O.S.)
                "Some Lebo kids jumped him outside the
                O." "It was some kids from North Hills."
                "That's not what I heard."

        Brad moves into the arms of CHARLOTTE (18), cheerleader cute.
        As Brad kisses her, Charlie sees Patrick down the hall,
        watching them. Patrick closes his locker. Hurting.

                          CHARLIE
                Are you okay?

                          PATRICK
                Not now, Charlie. I'm sorry.

        Patrick storms off.

126   INT. CAFETERIA - LUNCH   126

        Charlie sits at his table, alone. He watches Patrick leave
        the lunch line, passing a chorus of...

                          TWIN SENIOR GIRLS

Patrick says nothing. He's too sad to fight the mob today.
He just moves to his table when the Nose Tackle sticks out
his leg. Patrick falls on his tray. The kids laugh.

                    NOSE TACKLE
          Oops. Sorry, Nothing.

Patrick smiles to himself, dusts off, and turns to Brad.

                    PATRICK
          You going to do something?

                    BRAD HAYS
          What are you talking about?

                    PATRICK
          Your pet ape just tripped me. Are you
          going to say something?

                    BRAD HAYS
          Why would I?

                    PATRICK
          You know why.

It's too far. Brad can feel people staring.

                    BRAD HAYS
          This is pathetic, man. Your fixation on
          me.

Brad's friends laugh. Patrick's eyes narrow.

                    PATRICK
          Do you want your friends to know how you
          got those bruises? Really?

                    BRAD HAYS
          I got jumped in a parking lot.

                    PATRICK
          Where? In Schenley Park? Do they know
          about Schenley Park?
              (to Brad's friends)
          Do you guys know about Schenley Park?

Brad stands and gets right in Patrick's face.

                    BRAD HAYS
          I don't know what kind of sick shit
          you're trying to pull.
              (real warning)
          But you better walk away now... Nothing.

                    PATRICK
          Fine. Say hi to your dad for me.

Patrick turns and leaves. And then, as an afterthought...

                    BRAD HAYS
          Whatever... faggot.

Brad's friends laugh. Patrick stops and turns. Last chance.

                    PATRICK
          What did you call me?

                    BRAD HAYS
          I called you a faggo--

Smack.

Before Brad can even finish, Patrick throws a vicious right
to the cheek. Brad tackles him. And the two start fighting.
The cafeteria erupts in NOISE.

                    PATRICK
          Say that shit again! Say that shit
          again!

Brad's football buddies rise and peel Patrick off Brad. Mary
Elizabeth and Sam jump up from their corner table.

                    MARY ELIZABETH
          It's Patrick!

The cafeteria gets louder. The Nose Tackle holds Patrick up.
More Noise. The Linebacker hits Patrick in the face.

                    SAM
          No! No!

Sam rushes up and the Nose Tackle pushes her down. She lands
on her tail bone. Thud. Patrick gets hit a couple of times
in the face. The kids cheer the fight. It's getting louder
and louder with more and more noise. And then...

                                        SMASH CUT TO:

Silence.

Charlie comes out from a blink. He calmly looks around. For
a moment, he doesn't understand where he is. He looks up.
All the kids are staring at him. Mary Elizabeth. Alice.
Brad. They are all quiet. Afraid of him. Charlie looks at
his hand, clenched in a fist. It is already covered with...

Charlie's confused until he sees the Linebacker holding his
broken, bloody nose. He's looking at Charlie...

Terrified.

The image pans over. The Nose Tackle is on the ground.
Charlie stands over them. He is disconnected. It's an out
of body experience. He reaches out and helps Patrick to his
feet. Then, he calmly turns and stares right through Brad.

                    CHARLIE
               (icy calm)
          If you touch my friends again, I'll blind
          you.

Brad is stunned. So is everyone... except Sam.

127   INT. PRINCIPAL'S OFFICE - AFTERNOON   127

Charlie sits in the waiting room of the principal's office.
He looks through the glass where Principal Small talks to
Brad. After a beat, she pats Brad's shoulder and opens the
door. Leaving Charlie and Brad alone in the waiting room.
Just as Brad is about to leave...

                    BRAD HAYS
          Charlie?

                    CHARLIE
          Yeah?

                    BRAD HAYS
          Thanks for stopping them.

                    CHARLIE
          Sure, Brad.

Brad doesn't look at him. He just moves on.

128   EXT. MILL GROVE HIGH SCHOOL - PARKING LOT - AFTERNOON   128

Charlie exits the building. Kids stare at him. Then, look
away. Charlie feels very lost until he sees... Sam. She
smiles. It brings him back instantly. And then, gently...

                    SAM
          How you doing, Charlie?

                    CHARLIE
          I don't know. I keep trying, but... I
          can't really remember what I did.

Sam can see he's afraid of himself. She nods, sympathetic.

                    SAM
Do you want me to tell you?

                    CHARLIE
          (scared)
Yeah.

                    SAM
You saved my brother. That's what you
did.

                    CHARLIE
So, you're not scared of me?

                    SAM
No.

                    CHARLIE
And can we be friends again?

                    SAM
Of course.

The minute she hugs him, the numb goes away. She kisses the
top of his head and puts her arm around his shoulder. They
begin walking away.

                    SAM (CONT'D)
Come on. Let's go be psychos together.

129 INT. PATRICK AND SAM'S HOUSE - KITCHEN - NIGHT   129

Mary Elizabeth looks at us because she wants us to know...

                    MARY ELIZABETH
I'm dating Peter now.

She motions to **PETER**. College. Glasses. Good looking-ish.

                    MARY ELIZABETH (CONT'D)
He's in college with Craig. He's
opinionated, and we have intellectual
debates. You were very sweet, but our
relationship was too one-sided. I know
this is hard for you.

                    CHARLIE
I'm just glad you're happy.

                    MARY ELIZABETH
Okay.

Mary Elizabeth joins Peter. Charlie looks at his friends.

that says, "They forget. I don't." After a beat, Patrick comes downstairs. He looks sad with his bruises.

> PATRICK
> Hey Craig, Sam will be down soon.

> MARY ELIZABETH
> We're going to miss the movie.

> CRAIG
> Yeah, I'll go put some pep in her step.

As Craig moves upstairs, Patrick approaches Charlie.

> PATRICK
> Hey... you wanna get out of here?

> CHARLIE
> Sure, Patrick.

130   EXT. WEST END OVERLOOK - NIGHT   130

Patrick drives Sam's truck up the hill to the overlook.

> PATRICK (V.O.)
> I'll tell you something, Charlie. I feel
> good. You know what I mean? Maybe
> tomorrow I'll take you to this karaoke
> place downtown. And this club off the
> strip. They don't card. And the
> Schenley Park scene. You gotta see the
> "fruit loop" at least one time.

131   EXT. WEST END OVERLOOK - NIGHT   131

Charlie and Patrick walk the lighted path, howling at the moon. Patrick holds a thermos, filled with who knows what.

> PATRICK
> Oh, my God. My life is officially an
> after school special. Son of a bitch!

> CHARLIE
> (laughing)
> It kind of is. It so is.

More laughter. They arrive at the lookout. They drink.

> PATRICK
> So, you ever hear the one about Lily
> Miller?

> CHARLIE
> I don't know.

                    PATRICK
          Really? I thought your brother would
          have told you. It's a classic.

                    CHARLIE
          Maybe.

                    PATRICK
          So, Lily comes here with this guy Parker.
          And this was going to be the night they
          were going to lose their virginity. So,
          she did it really proper. She packed a
          picnic. Stole a bottle of wine.
          Everything was perfect, and they're just
          about to 'do it' when they realize they
          forgot the condoms. So, what do you
          think happened?

                    CHARLIE
          I don't know.

                    PATRICK
          They did it with one of the sandwich
          bags.

They start laughing and screaming.

                    CHARLIE
          Ew! That's disgusting!

                    PATRICK
          Yes! It is! Let's keep the train
          rolling. Suburban legends. Charlie!

Patrick points to Charlie, who thinks...

                    CHARLIE
          Uh. Well... there was this girl named
          Second Base Stace. She had boobs in the
          4th grade--

                    PATRICK
          Mosquito bites. Promising. Go.

                    CHARLIE
          And she let some of the boys feel them.

                    PATRICK
          That's your suburban legend? Did you at
          least cop a feel?

                    CHARLIE
          No.

> PATRICK
> Of course not. You went home, listened
> to "Asleep," wrote a poem about her self-
> esteem--

> CHARLIE
> Fine! Okay. Your turn.

Patrick walks over and sits down next to Charlie.

> PATRICK
> Yeah, I've got one. Well, there was this
> one guy. Queer as a 3 dollar bill.
> Guy's father didn't know about his son.
> So, he comes down into the basement one
> night when he's supposed to be out of
> town. Catches his son with another boy.
> So, he starts beating him. But not like
> the slap kind. Like the real kind. And
> the boyfriend says, "Stop. You're
> killing him." And the son just yells
> "Get out." And eventually the boyfriend
> just did.

Patrick stops. Gripped by sad. He can't shake.

> PATRICK (CONT'D)
> Why can't you save anybody?

> CHARLIE
> I don't know.

> PATRICK
> Forget it. I'm free now, right? I could
> meet the love of my life any second now.
> Things will be different now, and that's
> good. I just need to meet a good guy.

> CHARLIE
> Yeah.

Patrick looks at him. Charlie has never seen him so
vulnerable. After a beat... Patrick kisses Charlie on the
mouth. Unsure of what to do, Charlie lets it happen. His
eyes open the whole time. A moment, then Patrick looks at
Charlie. He collapses into his chest.

> PATRICK
> I'm sorry.

> CHARLIE
> It's alright.

Charlie holds his friend as Patrick begins to cry. And we leave them, the city lights small in the distance.

132   EXT. CITY HIGHWAY - NIGHT   132

We see the truck glide down the highway.

                    CHARLIE (V.O.)
              I've been spending a lot of time with
              Patrick. He begins every night really
              excited.

133   EXT. SCHENLEY PARK - NIGHT   133

Patrick and Charlie are parked at the entrance of Schenley Park. Patrick speaks, very animated, until...

                    CHARLIE (V.O.)
              He always says he feels free, and tonight
              is his destiny. But after awhile, he
              runs out of things to keep himself numb.

... the words leave him, and we can see how sad he really is.

134   INT. SAM AND PATRICK'S HOUSE - MOMENTS LATER   134

Patrick hands Sam an envelope. Sam holds it. Pins and needles.

                    CHARLIE (V.O.)
              Then, Sam got her letter from Penn State.

Sam opens the letter. She reads. Tears instantly well up in her eyes. She leaves the room and walks down the hall. Patrick picks up the letter.

                    PATRICK
                  (reading)
              "We will require you to take our summer
              session at the main campus immediately
              following your high school graduation."
                  (off Charlie's look)
              She got in, Charlie.

Charlie turns back to Sam. She holds him with sweet relief and redemption.

135   INT. CAFETERIA - DAY   135

Charlie laughs with his friends in the cafeteria.

                    CHARLIE (V.O.)
              After that all Patrick could talk about

                           CHARLIE (V.O.) (CONT'D)
            did get into NYU Film School. Patrick is
            going to the University of Washington
            because he wants to be near the music in
            Seattle.

136   INT. SHOP CLASS - DAY   136

Charlie and a group of students stand, looking up at the
wall, which is covered with...

                           CHARLIE (V.O.)
            But he wasn't going to leave without
            organizing the best senior prank ever.

... <u>All</u> <u>The</u> <u>Shop</u> <u>Tools</u> <u>Painted</u> <u>Pink</u>

The shop teacher, Mr. Callahan stares at the wall, furious.
As the students gawk, Charlie smiles to himself.

137   INT. CAFETERIA - LUNCH   137

Sam and the girls chat excitedly. Summer is almost here.

                           CHARLIE (V.O.)
            Sam is going to leave right after
            graduation. It all feels very exciting;
            I just wish it were happening to me.

138   INT. CHARLIE'S BEDROOM - DAY   138

Charlie sits on his bed, finishing the letter.

                           CHARLIE
            Especially because ever since I blacked
            out in the cafeteria, it's been getting
            worse. And I can't turn it off this
            time.

Charlie puts down the letter.

139   INT. BILL'S CLASSROOM - MORNING   139

The kids pass their copies of <u>The Great Gatsby</u> up to the
front, where Bill collects them for next year's freshmen.
The class is buzzing loud.

                           BILL
            Guys, you want to pass your copies of
            Gatsby up to the front please? And I
            know it's the last day, but if we could
            just keep it to a dull roar, I'd
            appreciate it.

The class quiets down.

> BILL (CONT'D)
> Thank you for such a great year. I had a
> blast. I hope you did, too. And I hope
> you have a great time this summer on your
> vacations. Now, who here is going to be
> reading for pleasure this summer?

Charlie looks to see if anyone is watching... then, decides
to raise his hand anyway. Bill is proud.

> BILL (CONT'D)
> Very good, Charlie. Who else?

Charlie looks at the Smart Ass Freshman who tormented him all
year. She sighs. Nothing left to say to him.

140   INT. BILL'S CLASSROOM - LATER   140

The last kids exit the classroom. Charlie walks down the
aisle and stands in front of Bill.

> BILL
> Last day.

> CHARLIE
> Yeah. So, uh, I know it's none of my
> business, but have you decided... are you
> going to New York?

> BILL
> Well, my wife and I like it here, and I
> think I might be better at teaching than
> writing.

Charlie is relieved. Bill is staying.

> BILL (CONT'D)
> So, uh Charlie... I was thinking maybe I
> could still give you books next year.

> CHARLIE
> Yeah. Yeah.

> BILL
> I think you could write one of them one
> day.

> CHARLIE
>   (fragile belief)
> Really?

> BILL
> I do.

Charlie is quiet. Then...

                    CHARLIE
          You're the best teacher I ever had.

                    BILL
          Thank you.

He gives Bill a shy sideways hug. The two men say nothing
else. Charlie waves and leaves. Bill smiles to himself.

141   INT. MILL GROVE HIGH SCHOOL - HALLWAY - AFTERNOON   141

Times Square has nothing on these seniors. Charlie watches
the gang on their last day of high school. When the clock
hits 10 seconds to 3pm, all the students chant...

                    SAM & COMPANY
          10-9-8-7-6-5-4-3-2...

                    STUDENT (O.S.)
          Oh, my God, get me the hell out of here!

                    ALL
               1!

They all cheer and hug each other. Patrick loses his mind
with joy and charges down the hallway.

                                        SMASH CUT TO:

142   EXT. MILL GROVE FOOTBALL STADIUM - SUNSET   142

A brilliant sunset. We see the gang. In silhouette.
Running up the bleachers after the sun.

                    CHARLIE (V.O.)
          Dear Friend... I wanted to tell you about
          us running. There was this beautiful
          sunset. And just a few hours before,
          everyone I love had their last day of
          high school ever. And I was happy
          because they were happy, even though I
          counted, and I have 1,095 days to go.

143   INT. CHARLIE'S HOUSE - FIREPLACE - LATE AFTERNOON   143

Prom night. Charlie sees Candace posing for Dad's camera.
For a moment, we think Candace went to prom with Derek.

                    CHARLIE (V.O.)
          I kept thinking about what school was
          going to be like without them as they

As mom and dad move out of the way, we realize Candace is
standing with her 3 best girlfriends. They look beautiful.

>   CHARLIE (V.O.) (CONT'D)
>   My sister finally decided to break up
>   with Derek and go stag with her
>   girlfriends instead.

144   EXT. SAM AND PATRICK'S HOUSE - SUNSET   144

Prom night continues. The antique limo is so garish, it's
great. Charlie snaps pictures with Sam's mom and Patrick's
dad. Mary Elizabeth is with her boyfriend, Peter. Alice
stands with Patrick, dashing in his Mod Suit Tux.

>   CHARLIE (V.O.)
>   And then there was Sam...

The image moves to the front of the house, where Sam emerges.
She wears a vintage flapper dress from the 20's. Radiant.

>   CHARLIE (V.O.) (CONT'D)
>   I've looked at her pictures since that
>   night. I like to see how happy she was
>   before she knew.

Sam joins Craig. They kiss for the cameras, then run with
the rest of the gang to the limosine.

>   CHARLIE (V.O.) (CONT'D)
>   They were in a hotel suite after prom
>   when the truth came out...

The gang poses for more pictures in front of the limo.

>   CHARLIE (V.O.) (CONT'D)
>   Basically, Craig has been cheating on Sam
>   the whole time. When I heard that, I
>   kept thinking about the happy girl in
>   these pictures. Because she doesn't have
>   1,095 days to go.

145   EXT. PARKING LOT - AFTERNOON   145

Graduation Day. The place is packed with graduating seniors
and families. Charlie's mom and dad fawn over Candace with
the video camera. Charlie finally finds... Sam.

>   CHARLIE (V.O.)
>   She made it. This is her time. And no
>   one should be able to take that away.

They approach each other and hug.

                    CHARLIE (CONT'D)
          Congratulations.

                    PATRICK
          Oh, Charlie's here! Guys, group photo!
          We should all take a group photo. Get
          against the railing and try to look
          suave!

The kids line up for the picture they will always remember.

                    PATRICK (CONT'D)
          Yeah, this is the one. That's going to
          be a great angle.

Patrick bows to reveal the top of his cap reads, "Nothing
Hates You." The parents line up cameras. "Cheese!" Snap.

                                             SMASH CUT TO:

146   INT. SAM AND PATRICK'S KITCHEN/LIVING ROOM - NIGHT   146

The grandfather clock reads 9:30pm. The room is festive
under streamers wishing Sam luck at Penn State. The kids
sign each other's yearbooks. Charlie sees Sam smile at old
photos. He misses her already.

                    CHARLIE (V.O.)
          At her going away party, I wanted her to
          know about that night we went through the
          tunnel. And how for the first time, I
          felt like I belonged somewhere.

                                             CUT TO:

147   INT. SAM AND PATRICK'S KITCHEN/LIVING ROOM - LATER   147

10:28pm. Charlie doesn't know where the time keeps going.
Sam opens goodbye presents from her friends.

                    CHARLIE (V.O.)
          And tomorrow, she's leaving. So, I
          wanted to give her a part of me.

Charlie watches Sam pick up his present. She carefully peels
the tape to reveal that Charlie gave her all of his books.

                    SAM
          Are these all your books, Charlie?

He nods. They lock eyes and do not speak.

148   INT. SAM'S BEDROOM - NIGHT   148

The pictures are down. The dressers empty. The suitcase is
open on the bed. Charlie watches Sam fold clothes and put
them in her suitcase. He has promised himself he will not
cry. Even when she packs away his Beatles 45 of "Something."

Instead, he looks at her and tries to remember every detail.
Her hair and brown eyes and sound of her voice.

                    SAM
          Thanks for staying up with me.

                    CHARLIE
          Sure. My brother said Penn State has a
          restaurant called Ye Olde College Diner.
          You have to get a grilled stickie on your
          first night. It's a tradition.

                    SAM
          That sounds like fun.

                    CHARLIE
          Yeah. Pretty soon, you'll have a whole
          new group of friends, and you won't even
          think about this place anymore.

                    SAM
          Yes, I will.

Sam moves some suitcases over to the pile in the room. They
stand next to each other. Close.

                    SAM (CONT'D)
          I had lunch with Craig today.

                    CHARLIE
          Yeah?

                    SAM
          He said he was sorry, and that I was
          right to break up with him. But I'm
          driving away, and I just felt so small.
          Just asking myself why do I and everyone
          I love pick people who treat us like
          we're nothing?

                    CHARLIE
          We accept the love we think we deserve.

He says it sober. Without judgement. Sam lets it sink in.
Charlie walks over to the bed to do more packing. Then, she
turns to him.

                    SAM
          Then, why didn't you ever ask me out?

Charlie didn't expect that. He is silent. Heart pounding.

                    CHARLIE
          I, uh, I just didn't think you wanted
          that.

                    SAM
          Well, what did you want?

                    CHARLIE
          I just want you to be happy.

                    SAM
          Don't you get it, Charlie? I can't feel
          that. It's really sweet and everything,
          but you can't just sit there and put
          everybody's lives ahead of yours and
          think that counts as love. I don't want
          to be somebody's crush. I want people to
          like the real me.

                    CHARLIE
          I know who you are, Sam.

Sam waits. And Charlie finally speaks from the heart.

                    CHARLIE (CONT'D)
          I know I'm quiet, and I know I should
          speak more, but if you knew the things
          that were in my head most of the time,
          you'd know what it really meant. How
          much we are alike. And how we've been
          through the same things. And you're not
          small. You're beautiful.

He can't contain himself anymore. He moves to her and kisses
her. They stand. Move to the bed. Kissing. Charlie's
heart pounds. They sit on the bed. Still kissing.

We see her fingertips. Her hand on Charlie's knee. When she
touches him, Charlie pulls away from her. Shocked. Like
he's seen a ghost. It hits Charlie like freezing water.

                    SAM
          What's wrong, Charlie?

                    CHARLIE
          Oh, ah... nothing.

Charlie shakes off whatever was bothering him and continues

149   EXT. SAM AND PATRICK'S HOUSE - MORNING   149

It's like a dream for Charlie. He watches Sam hug Alice and Mary Elizabeth goodbye. But Charlie is somewhere else.

               SAM
     I'll call all the time.

               MARY ELIZABETH
   Promise.

               SAM
   And we'll all see each other in New York.

               SAM'S MOM
  Come on, Sam.

Charlie can't take it. He moves to the side of the truck and puts in the last suitcase. He looks over at Sam.

                       SMASH CUT TO:

150   INT. SAM'S BEDROOM - NIGHT   150

QUICK FLASH... Charlie remembers kissing Sam the night before. Her hand touches Charlie's knee.

                     BACK TO PRESENT:

151   EXT. SAM AND PATRICK'S HOUSE - MORNING   151

Charlie snaps himself out of it. He turns back as Mary Elizabeth and Alice part ways. Charlie locks eyes with Sam. They take a moment. And then they come together to hug. She kisses him goodbye, trying not to cry.

After a moment, Sam climbs into the driver's seat of her truck with Patrick riding shotgun. Charlie looks dazed.

                     SMASH CUT TO:

152   INT. SAM'S BEDROOM - NIGHT   152

QUICK FLASH... Charlie remembers pulling away from Sam. Shocked. Like he's seen a ghost.

               SAM
   What's wrong, Charlie?

                     BACK TO PRESENT:

153   EXT. SAM AND PATRICK'S HOUSE - MORNING   153

Sam starts the truck. Charlie wants to scream for her to
stop. But he's frozen. She drives away. He watches her go.
The truck gets smaller in the distance until it turns at the
stop sign. And disappears. Charlie stands there, alone.

                                              SMASH CUT TO:

154   INT. SAM'S BEDROOM - NIGHT   154

QUICK FLASH... Charlie remembers the night with Sam. We see
her put her hand on his knee. The image moves up the arm.
To the shoulder. To the face. And we reveal, we are not in
Sam's bedroom. And it is not Sam touching Charlie. But...

Aunt Helen

                         AUNT HELEN
                 Don't wake your sister.

                                              BACK TO REALITY:

155   EXT. SAM AND PATRICK'S HOUSE - MORNING   155

The memory only registers as a small blink of his eye.
Charlie sees his friends are crying. He's not. He's numb.

156   EXT. SUBURBAN STREET - MORNING   156

Charlie walks down the street. His eyes far away. The
images and memories are short, violent bursts. If you've
never had an anxiety attack, this is how it feels.

157   EXT. CHARLIE'S STREET - NIGHT (FLASHBACK)   157

QUICK FLASH. It's Christmas Eve. Aunt Helen smiles to
Little Charlie.

                         AUNT HELEN
                 It'll be our little secret, okay?

Little Charlie nods.

158   EXT. SUBURBAN STREET - MORNING (PRESENT)   158

BACK TO PRESENT. Charlie walks toward us on the sidewalk.
We see him through a long lens. His image fractures. We see
him in different planes of the image. He's beginning to
break apart. One image. Two images.

159   INT. CHARLIE'S LIVING ROOM - NIGHT (FLASHBACK)   159

QUICK FLASH.   Little Candace is asleep on the floor.   Aunt
Helen sits next to Little Charlie on the sofa.

                          AUNT HELEN
                Look, Charlie. She's fast asleep.

160   EXT. SUBURBAN STREET - MORNING (PRESENT)   160

BACK TO PRESENT.   We see Charlie fracturing.   The pieces
scattered.   Out of focus.   Lost.   He's all over the frame.

161   INT. CHARLIE'S LIVING ROOM - NIGHT (FLASHBACK)   161

QUICK FLASH.   Aunt Helen points to Little Candace.

                          AUNT HELEN
                Don't wake your sister.

162   INT. CHARLIE'S HOUSE - DAY (PRESENT)   162

BACK TO PRESENT.   Charlie enters his house.

                                                SMASH CUT TO:

163   INT. AUNT HELEN'S CAR - NIGHT (FLASHBACK)   163

QUICK FLASH.   Aunt Helen gets hit by the semi-truck.

164   INT. ENTRY HALL - NIGHT (FLASHBACK)   164

QUICK FLASH.   Little Charlie's mom opens the door to reveal a
policeman.

165   INT. CHARLIE'S HOUSE - DAY (PRESENT)   165

BACK TO PRESENT.   Charlie is in the same entry hall in the
same house 8 years later.   Banging his head against the wall.
"It's my fault.   It's all my fault."

He passes the photo wall on the stairs.   We see the images of
the family.   Church.   Communion.   Baby pictures.   Years of
history staring at us.   Ghosts on the wall.

166   INT. CHARLIE'S BEDROOM - DAY (PRESENT)   166

BACK TO PRESENT.   Charlie sits at his desk.   We see him from
behind.   Perfectly still.   Trying to keep himself calm.

                          CHARLIE
                Stop crying.

167   INT. VARIOUS LOCATIONS - DAY (FLASHBACK)   167

QUICK FLASH. Charlie thinks everyone is staring at him. His
sister and her friends. His brother and mother. Mary
Elizabeth and Alice. And worst of all... Sam and Patrick the
night they toasted him. A paranoid nightmare.

168   INT. CHARLIE'S BEDROOM - DAY (PRESENT)   168

BACK TO PRESENT. Charlie's falling to pieces. The tears run
down his face.

                         CHARLIE
              Stop crying.

169   INT. VARIOUS LOCATIONS - VARIOUS TIMES (FANTASY)   169

QUICK FLASH. Derek hits Candace. Patrick hits Brad. The
cafeteria erupts into violence.

And Charlie remembers what he's blacked out.

We see him in the cafeteria. Terrifying. He thinks he sees
Aunt Helen as he breaks the Linebacker's nose. Hits another
in the throat. And pushes another. Charlie looks at his
hand, covered in blood. The whole school staring at him.

170   INT. CHARLIE'S BEDROOM - DAY (PRESENT)   170

BACK TO PRESENT. Charlie holds his head. Trying to stuff
the pictures back in his brain. But he can't. They keep
coming and coming, faster and faster. Sam's hand, Little
Charlie on top of the stairs, the police telling him Aunt
Helen is dead.

                       CHARLIE (V.O.)
              It'll be our little secret.

We go behind his head. The image moves closer and closer.
Until it feels like we are inside Charlie's mind.

                                              SMASH CUT TO:

171   EXT. HOUSE SWIMMING POOL - DAY   171

We see Candace hanging out with her girlfriends at a friend's
backyard pool. Her **FRIEND** (18, pretty) holds the cordless.

                    CANDACE'S FRIEND
              Candace... your brother's on the phone.

Candace casually picks up the phone.

                    CANDACE
          Hello.

                    CHARLIE (V.O.)
          Hey, Candace.

                    CANDACE
          Charlie?

                    CHARLIE
          Sam and Patrick left, and um, I just
          can't stop thinking something.

                    CANDACE
          What?

                    CHARLIE
          Candace, I killed Aunt Helen, didn't I?
          She died getting my birthday present, so
          I guess I killed her, right? I've tried
          to stop thinking that, but I can't. She
          keeps driving away and dying over and
          over.

Candace looks like she got hit with ice water. She knows her
brother. She knows this voice. Candace covers the phone.

                    CANDACE
          Call the police and send them to my
          house.

                    CHARLIE
          And I can't stop her. I'm crazy again.

                    CANDACE
          No, Charlie, listen to me. Mom and dad
          are going to be home with Chris any
          second.

                    CHARLIE
          I was just thinking... what if I wanted
          her to die, Candace?

                    CANDACE
          What? Charlie... Charlie!

Dial tone.

172   INT. CHARLIE'S HOUSE - DAY   172

We begin in the house. It's silent. The hallway. The entry
hall. The empty bedroom. Charlie's typewriter on his desk.

It's all so quiet. And then, we see Charlie walking down the hallway. He turns the corner and enters the...

MATCH CUT TO:

173   INT. CHARLIE'S KITCHEN - DAY (PAST AND PRESENT)   173

Kitchen. One room. Charlie doesn't know where he is anymore. The past and present have bled together.

QUICK FLASH. We see Little Charlie turn the corner into the kitchen. BACK TO PRESENT as 16 year old Charlie stands in the same kitchen, breathing shallow.

QUICK FLASH. 7 year old Charlie walks up to Aunt Helen sitting at the kitchen table. BACK TO PRESENT as 16 year old Charlie begins to have a full blown anxiety attack.

QUICK FLASH. 7 year old Charlie takes Aunt Helen's hand and turns it over... <u>to reveal her wrist scars</u>.

BACK TO PRESENT as Charlie looks from the table to the counter with the bread and the KNIVES. He stares at the knives for a moment. Just as...

The Policemen break down the door.

SMASH CUT TO:

174   INT. HOSPITAL ROOM - NIGHT   174

We see Charlie's reflection in the window. The door opens slowly, and his psychiatrist, Dr. Burton, enters. She finds him sitting in the corner. He has been crying.

                    DR. BURTON
          Charlie? I'm Dr. Burton.

                    CHARLIE
          Where am I?

                    DR. BURTON
          Mayview hospital.

This news hits Charlie hard. He begins to panic.

                    CHARLIE
          You have to let me go. My dad can't
          afford it.

                    DR. BURTON
          Don't worry about that.

                    CHARLIE
          No. I saw them when I was little. And I
          don't want to be a Mayview kid. Just
          tell me how to stop it.

                    DR. BURTON
          Stop what?

                    CHARLIE
          Seeing it. All their lives. All the
          time. Just... how do you stop seeing it?

                    DR. BURTON
          Seeing what, Charlie?

Charlie breaks.

                    CHARLIE
          There is so much pain. And I don't know
          how to not notice it.

                    DR. BURTON
          What's hurting you?

                    CHARLIE
          No! Not me. It's them. It's everyone.
          It never stops. Do you understand?

Dr. Burton smiles, sympathetic. Charlie nods, relieved that
someone finally understands. Until...

                    DR. BURTON
          What about your Aunt Helen?

Like cold water. What was tears is now confusion and soon to
be shame. Dr. Burton is gentle to him.

                    CHARLIE
          What about her?

                    DR. BURTON
          Can you see her?

                    CHARLIE
          Yes, she had a terrible life. But... I
          mean, what am I...

                    DR. BURTON
          You said some things about her in your
          sleep.

                    CHARLIE
          I don't care.

> DR. BURTON
> If you want to get better, you have to--

Charlie looks at her, nodding her encouragement.

> CHARLIE
> She was... insane.

The minute he says one word of truth, he feels ashamed. He stops talking. Dr. Burton does not press him. Not today.

> DR. BURTON
> Charlie, are you going to let me help you here?

Charlie cries and nods.

> CHARLIE
> Okay.

> DR. BURTON
> Do you remember anything before you blacked out?

> CHARLIE
> I, uh... I remember leaving Sam's house, and walking home...

We move away from them as Charlie's voice trails off.

175   INT. HOSPITAL ROOM - MORNING   175

The sun creeps through the windows. We can hear birds outside. The intercom is quiet. Charlie is alone. He looks at Sam's typewriter. "Dear Friend" is already typed.

> CHARLIE (V.O.)
> I was in the hospital for awhile. I won't go into detail about all of it. But I will say there were some very bad days. And some unexpected beautiful days.

Charlie picks up a get well card from Sam.

176   INT. HOSPITAL HALLWAY - DAY   176

Dr. Burton walks Charlie's parents down the hallway.

> CHARLIE (V.O.)
> The worst day was the time my doctor told my mom and dad what Aunt Helen did to me.

In the distance, we see Charlie's mom and dad stop. Shocked.

177   INT. HOSPITAL ROOM - DAY   177

Charlie looks up and sees his mom and dad in the doorway.

                    MOTHER
          Honey?

His mother comes to hold him.

                    MOTHER (CONT'D)
          I'm so sorry.

For a second, we see the emotion his father hides behind the
sports page, before he chokes it down. He walks over to his
son and kisses his forehead.

178   INT. HOSPITAL ROOM - MORNING   178

Charlie, Chris, and Candace sit on the bed, playing cards.

                    CHARLIE (V.O.)
          The best days were those when I could
          have visitors. My brother and sister
          always came for those until Chris had to
          go to training camp. He's going to be
          first string this year. And my sister
          told me she met a nice guy at her summer
          job.

179   INT. HOSPITAL HALLWAY - AFTERNOON   179

Charlie leaves his room with his suitcase in hand. His
mother waits in the hallway with Dr. Burton.

                    DR. BURTON
          There he is. So, I'll see you Thursday
          at 6, right?

Charlie nods and leaves the hospital with his mother.

                    CHARLIE (V.O.)
          My doctor said we can't choose where we
          can come from, but we can choose where we
          go from there. I know it's not all the
          answers, but it was enough to start
          putting these pieces together.

Dr. Burton smiles, then turns back into the hospital.

180   INT. CHARLIE'S DINING ROOM - NIGHT   180

The family sits at the dinner table.

                         FATHER
          God bless this food that we are about to
          receive. We thank You for this bounty in
          the name of our Lord Jesus Christ. Amen.

After they say "Amen," the room falls silent. The family is
on pins and needles. No one touches their food. Until...

                         CHARLIE
          How do you think the Penguins are going
          to do this year, dad?

                         FATHER
          God damn Penguins. I think they're
          allergic to God damn defense.

                         CHARLIE
          What do the players call a puck again?

                         FATHER
          A biscuit.

                         CANDACE
          Are you sure it's not a "God damn
          biscuit?"

                         FATHER
          You're cruisin' for a bruisin'.

As things return to normal, dad picks up his paper. Candace
talks about the books she'll need for college. Everyone
starts eating. And Charlie smiles, happy to just be home.

181 INT. CHARLIE'S HOUSE - DUSK   181

Ding dong. The door opens to reveal Patrick, smiling.

                         PATRICK
          Can Charlie come out and play?

Charlie's mother smiles. Charlie smiles, too. Especially
when he sees... Sam. Standing next to Patrick. Her hair a
little different. Her eyes alive and happy.

182 INT. KINGS FAMILY RESTAURANT - NIGHT   182

The gang of three sit at their booth. Sam and Patrick have
their coffee. Charlie has his brownie. Like always.

                         SAM
          That first night, I had grilled stickies.
          It was so good. You have to visit in the
          Fall. We'll have some. Okay?

                    CHARLIE
          Definitely.

                    PATRICK
          Sorry, Sam. Charlie has a breakdown
          scheduled for October.

Charlie laughs. Sam smiles. After a beat...

                    SAM
          Well, can I tell you something? I've
          been away for two months. It's another
          world. And it gets better.
               (off Charlie's smile)
          And my roommate Katie has the best taste
          in music.

Sam puts a cassette tape down on the table.

                    SAM (CONT'D)
          I found the tunnel song.

Charlie looks at Sam and Patrick, who smile.

                    SAM (CONT'D)
          Let's drive.

183 EXT. KINGS FAMILY RESTAURANT - NIGHT   183

The three leave the restaurant and jump into Sam's truck.
Patrick drives. Charlie in the middle. Sam the passenger.

                    CHARLIE (V.O.)
          I don't know if I will have the time to
          write any more letters because I might be
          too busy trying to participate. So, if
          this does end up being the last letter, I
          just want you to know that I was in a bad
          place before I started high school. And
          you helped me.

184 INT. SAM'S TRUCK - NIGHT   184

The three friends are flying down the highway in Sam's truck.
The music blaring. The wind making their hair dance.

                    CHARLIE (V.O.)
          Even if you didn't know what I was
          talking about. Or know someone who's
          gone through it. It made me not feel
          alone.

With Sam's help, Charlie climbs through the little window

185   EXT. HIGHWAY 376 NORTH - NIGHT   185

Charlie gets into the back of the truck. He sits down,
looking back at the highway. Watching everywhere he's been.

                    CHARLIE (V.O.)
          Because I know there are people who say
          all of these things don't happen. And
          there are people who forget what it's
          like to be 16 when they turn 17.

We see Charlie in profile. The night sky behind him until...

186   INT. FORT PITT TUNNEL - NIGHT   186

... they enter the tunnel, and we realize just how fast
they're driving. The white tiles of the tunnel whiz by at
blinding speed. A perfect night. A perfect drive. Flying.

                    CHARLIE (V.O.)
          I know these will all be stories someday.
          And our pictures will become old
          photographs. And we'll all become
          somebody's mom or dad. But right now,
          these moments are not stories.

Charlie turns to face forward. To the moment. To Sam,
smiling at him from the front seat.

                    CHARLIE (V.O) (CONT'D)
          This is happening. I am here. And I am
          looking at her. And she is so beautiful.

Sam kisses Charlie. Then, she turns, and all three kids look
ahead to everything in front of them. Charlie begins to
stand in the back of the truck. Ready to leave the tunnel.

                    CHARLIE (V.O.) (CONT'D)
          I can see it. This one moment when you
          know you're not a sad story. You are
          alive. And as you stand up and see the
          lights on buildings and everything that
          makes you wonder. And you are listening
          to that song on that drive with the
          people you love most in this world.

Charlie stands in the back of the truck. The wind on his
face. He is free.

                    CHARLIE (V.O.) (CONT'D)
          And in this moment, I swear...

We see the moment as Charlie sees it. The tunnel's exit
getting bigger and brighter with the lights of the city
behind it.

                    CHARLIE (V.O.) (CONT'D)
          ... we are infinite.

The tunnel song blasts over the speakers as the truck flies
out of the tunnel. Sam and Patrick scream with excitement.
Charlie holds his arms in the air. The weight of the world
gone. If only for a moment. This one moment. We see the
city. A million lights like white stars in a glass dome. We
crane to the sky. We are in Heaven.

                                        FADE OUT.

Manufactured by Amazon.ca
Bolton, ON

29363370R00055